Touched by the Master

Other Books by
Fred and Florence Littauer

Freeing Your Mind From Memories That Bind
The Promise of Healing
Silver Boxes — The Gift of Encouragement
The Best of Florence Littauer
Blow Away the Black Clouds
After Every Wedding Comes a Marriage
Out of the Cabbage Patch
It Takes So Little to Be Above Average
The Gift of Encouraging Words
How to Get Along With Difficult People
Personality Plus
Personality Puzzle
Your Personality Tree
Dare to Dream
Testing 1...2...3
I've Found My Keys, Now Where's My Car?
Wake Up, Women!
Wake Up, Men!
Hope for Hurting Women
Looking for God in All the Right Places
Raising Christians Not Just Children
Put Power in Your Personality
Shades of Beauty

Christian Leaders and Speakers Seminar
(tape albums and manuals)

For additional information on the Christian Leaders and Speakers
Seminar (CLASS) and the Promise of Healing workshops, contact:

CLASS Speakers, Inc.
1645 S. Rancho Santa Fe Road
Suite 102
San Marcos, CA 92069
619-471-0233

Touched by the Master

FRED LITTAUER

CREATION HOUSE

Creation House
Strang Communications Company
600 Rinehart Road
Lake Mary, FL 32746
Phone: 407-333-3132
Fax: 407-333-7100
Web Site: http://www.strang.com

Incidents and persons portrayed in this volume are based on fact.
However, names and other details have been changed in some cases
to protect individuals' privacy.

Acknowledgments

For one who in high school and college hated to write and winced whenever a written assignment was given, writing this, my fifth book, has been an amazingly wonderful adventure.

This book has been such a pleasure and joy to write. First of all, the subject is so positive and uplifting, and second, the illustrations and experiences contributed by several others make such an important addition to the message — that our Lord Jesus Christ is alive! He has resurrected from the tomb! He hears our cries. He answers our askings, and He heals our hurts.

I wish to express my deepest appreciation to contributors who permitted their sometimes painful stories to be told. I wish I could identify them by their real names, for they deserve whatever recognition the Lord would have for them. However, to protect others who might be involved in their illustrations, names and places have been carefully obscured. Nevertheless, you may be assured all of these illustrations and contributions are true and have been lived as described.

To Paula Mitchell and Carol Miller, special sisters in Christ and valued members of our ministry team, I wish to express especial appreciation for your personal encouragement to me as well as your contributions to the message of this book.

Finally, to Sue Ann Jones and Deborah Poulalion, thank you for your diligent editorial work and encouragement as we prepared this manuscript for publication.

The eyes that have seen Jesus
will never see the same again.

The eyes that have looked
upon the Lord
will never look the same again.

Contents

Preface

OF JESUS APPEARED after His crucifixion as recorded in the Bible, and if the Lord Jesus is a living Lord, does it not follow that He could appear today at any time that He might choose or that we might ask?

In April 1993 my wife, Florence, and I were speaking at a weekend conference at the Christian Assembly Church in Columbus, Ohio. I asked from the platform, "How many of you have ever seen Jesus?" I expected a few hands might be raised. I was not prepared, however, for the vast sea of hands I saw before me. Fully one-third of those present raised a hand!

If this question were asked in a similar setting in your church, how many hands do you think would be raised? Would some say, "I don't understand the question"? Would they know what it means to see Jesus?

Preface

A few years ago a friend told us she had been to a conference where the speaker prayed and asked the Lord Jesus to manifest Himself to those in the audience. The speaker then asked those who had seen the Lord to raise their hands, and several people did!

At that time, the concept of seeing Jesus was totally outside my personal frame of reference or, as it is sometimes described, my comfort zone. However, because I am always eager to learn and never willing to discount someone else's spiritual experience simply because it is different from mine, I did the only logical thing. I opened my Bible. If an experience can be validated in the Scripture, I have no difficulty accepting it without question. I found numerous scriptural verifications that I will describe in chapter 3, as well as several others.

For the past ten years, the Lord has chosen to give me a ministry of healing through prayer to individuals who have suffered severe trauma in their childhoods. After realizing that the Lord Jesus would manifest Himself if we would ask it in prayer, I determined to ask Him to do so while I was praying with others. The very first person I prayed with in this manner promptly reported seeing herself alone but safe in a beautiful place. Soon she saw a figure and focused her spiritual eyesight on the person before her. It was the Lord Jesus Himself, who then beckoned her to "come to Me" as He began to minister His healing love to her!

Since that initial and amazingly rewarding experience, it has been a joyful practice for me and for those associated with our ministry as prayer directors to pray people into the presence of the Lord. The results have been life-changing and permanent. It has been thrilling to see the Master simply and effectively fulfill the promises He made to each of us in the Scripture. He is still teaching us anew about how He works and what He will do, especially in bringing healing for emotional hurts from our childhoods or adult lives.

Have *you* seen Jesus? Have you ever actually seen Him in the flesh so you could talk to Him as the disciples did and walk with Him and touch Him and even feel His loving arms around you? The Bible says you can! You can be touched by the Master.

1

The Encounter
in Nashville

$\mathcal{O}$NE SUMMER, FLORENCE and I were in Nashville, Tennessee, the world-renowned home of country music. We were not there to sing, play or be entertained. We had been invited to speak at the summer conference of a very large network marketing group. If I recall correctly, there were about three thousand wildly enthusiastic men and women there, all intent on building their own business networks. I am sure many of them will never forget that weekend because of all the information and motivation they received. I know now that the Lord had special plans for Florence and me in Nashville that we could never have anticipated. He also had plans for one other individual who, like a pebble thrown into a pond, has in turn affected numerous others and then others and then many, many more!

Here's how it all started. On Saturday morning of that weekend conference Florence was on stage in the Nashville Convention

Center, speaking to the entire group. She was giving her always enthusiastically-received message entitled Personality Plus, which is based on her best-selling book of the same name.

At each speaking event we set up a book table so the audience can purchase our books and tapes. After speaking, Florence likes to come out to the book table to greet people and to personally autograph books.

With such a large crowd, there was almost a mob scene at the book table after she finished speaking. People were eagerly try- ing to get up to the table to look at the resources we had available. Florence sat at a nearby table to meet those who wished to see her and to have her sign their books. Within only a few minutes there was a long and orderly line of folks waiting patiently for their opportunity.

Unbeknownst to us at that time, another little drama was play- ing out on the sideline. A young woman named Willa* came out of the meeting hall with her adult son at the same time as the others.[1] She yearned to meet Florence. *There was something about that lady who had been speaking on the stage,* she mused. *I should know that woman,* she thought to herself. *There's some- thing about her, something that makes me think I know her.* Willa mentioned her thoughts to her son, Tommy.**

"Why don't you just go and get in line and meet her then?" Tommy asked. "Maybe you do know her from somewhere. The only way you're going to find out is to ask her."

"No, Tommy, don't you understand? Do you see those people over there in that line? They've all bought books. They're wait- ing for her to autograph them. I don't have any money. I can't afford to buy even one book. I can't go over there and make a fool out of myself."

Willa had scraped together every penny she could find and then borrowed additional money to attend the conference and help pay for the hotel room she shared with three others. There was no way she could buy a book so she could talk to Florence,

* Not her real name
** Not his real name

and there was no way she was going to get in line without a book. The hopelessness of her situation overwhelmed her, and she ran sobbing to the ladies' room. Willa got there just in time to lose what little of her meager breakfast was still in her stomach.

At about three o'clock on Sunday afternoon Willa and Tommy and five friends packed into a van for the long drive through the night back home. The weekend had been a wonderful, uplifting experience for all of them, even Willa, despite her own momentary low point. They chatted and laughed and amused each other with stories of the weekend. There was no shortage of conversation. As the miles clicked by, however, one by one they got sleepy and dozed off. No wonder! Not one of them had gotten to bed before 3:30 A.M. on Sunday.

Around midnight Willa woke up, feeling wide awake. On the seat next to her was a copy of Florence's book *Dare to Dream* which one of her friends in the van had bought during the weekend. Turning on the dome light in the van, she started to read. A couple of the others stirred, but no one seemed to be awakened by the light. She read and read into the morning hours, fascinated by what she was seeing.

She came to the part where Florence was describing her own teenage years and the times she had spent at her grandmother's house on Clark Street, in Worcester, Massachusetts.

"That's it!" Willa shouted aloud.

"That's what?" her sleepy companions asked. "What are you talking about?"

"That's it! I knew I should know her! Her grandmother's house was on Clark Street in Worcester."

"Whose grandmother?" they asked in unison.

"Florence's, Florence Littauer's grandmother. She's the one who spoke about personalities on Saturday morning. I remember hearing my great-aunt talk about her mother's house on Clark Street in Worcester! From what she said, I think Florence's grandmother must be my great-grandmother. Florence and I are related! She's some kind of a distant cousin. There was something about her; I knew I should know her!"

When the conference concluded in Nashville, Florence and I flew home to Southern California. About three weeks later we received a letter at the office, which said in part:

> It's taken me a long time to get up the courage to write to you. You don't know me, but I was at the conference in Nashville and heard you both speak. I enjoyed your presentations so much and learned a lot from you. I wanted to meet you in the foyer near the book table, but the lines were so long and besides, I hadn't been able to buy a book. However, on the way home on Sunday night I woke up and picked up a copy of your book *Dare to Dream* that one of my friends had purchased. I read on and on for a couple of hours until I came to the part where you mentioned that your grandmother lived on Clark Street in Worcester, Massachusetts. I let out a scream right there in the van that woke up all my friends. "That's it!" I said. "She's related to me."
>
> You see, my great-aunt Martha's mother lived on Clark Street in Worcester, Massachusetts, too. That means we're related somehow — distant cousins, I guess. I just wanted to let you know in case you're ever in this area. I'd love to come and meet you. But I know you're a very busy person, and if you don't have time, that's OK, too. I would surely understand.

Always being interested in meeting long-lost relatives, I immediately picked up the phone to call Willa. No one answered, but I left our home number on the answering machine and asked Willa to call us that evening, if possible, as it was one of the rare nights we would actually be home.

Willa told us later that she was stunned when she got home from work to find my message on her answering machine. She said she never expected anyone as "important" as Florence to "waste her time" calling someone as "insignificant" as Willa. She was afraid to call us back because she feared she would be "blown off," and she knew she couldn't handle the rejection. Willa nervously waited until after supper. When her husband had gone off to his bowling league, she watched the clock until she thought it would be a good time to call.

So terrified was she of the reaction she might get, Willa told us, that she put on her old robe and slippers and went inside the bedroom closet with the telephone! She shut the door and sat on the floor. She couldn't take the chance that anyone might see her get turned down.

At about six-thirty, the phone rang at our home in California. "Cheerful greetings! This is Fred speaking," I answered in my usual manner.

Back in the closet, Willa felt a rush of relief. Maybe this wasn't going to be so threatening after all.

I called to Florence to pick up the phone in the kitchen, "It's Willa!" The three of us chatted for a good ten minutes and actually had a delightful time piecing together the missing parts of the puzzle of Florence and Willa's shared ancestry.

"Willa, we're going to be in Philadelphia in two weeks. Florence will be speaking at another networking function. If it's convenient for you to come over, we'd love to meet you. And if you'd like, perhaps you could help me at the book table."

I surprised even myself by this suggestion for her to help at the book table. When several hundred eager buyers hit the book table all at once, the last thing I need is an inexperienced and frightened woman trying to help me and getting in the way!

I told Willa where we would be and said if she could come she should just look for me at the book table. I would be setting it up early Friday afternoon and would be there most of the weekend until the conference was over.

When we arrived at our hotel in Philadelphia two weeks later, a message was waiting for us. Willa said she would be over about three o'clock Friday afternoon, and, if I would like, she would be glad to help set up the book table. Now that was an offer I couldn't refuse. Setting up the books for these big functions is a three-hour, backbreaking job. In addition to helping me set up, her work would give her a chance to get familiar with our books and tapes and prices.

Three o'clock Friday afternoon, right on schedule, a smartly-dressed woman in a dark business suit, walked up to me, stuck out her hand and said, "You must be Fred. I'm Willa." It was the beginning of an incredible saga that hasn't ended yet.

Willa worked with me all Friday afternoon and evening until quite late. She finally had a chance to meet her distant cousin Florence and to spend some personal time with her. When it was time for Willa to leave, she asked me if I would like her to come back the next day. She had purposely cleared her Saturday, hoping I might want her back! Willa has a take-charge personality, and she didn't need to be told anything twice. Although she didn't know the prices, she was a big help, and I was happy to have her back on Saturday.

I didn't realize it at the time, but Willa was not able to add up the prices of the books in her head, even though everything was in even dollars and there was no sales tax to figure. I didn't notice it at the time because I didn't really expect a new helper to know the prices anyway. I just asked her to show me the books being purchased, and in a second I could tell her the total amount due. This worked very well.

There was a reason why Willa couldn't add, but we didn't know it until almost a year later. She was dyslexic.[2] She couldn't have added the prices in her head even if she had known them. The good news is that Willa is no longer dyslexic! I'll tell you how she was healed a little later.

Willa worked with me from early Saturday morning until quite late Saturday night when we shut down the book table. Not only had she worked hard and effectively, she was also a lot of fun. We had some time in the afternoon for all three of us to get better acquainted. As we parted that night, I thanked Willa profusely for all her help and gave her a hundred-dollar bill as tangible evidence of my appreciation. She thanked me for allowing her to help and said she didn't want to accept the money. Willa is a strong personality, but I am also. She did take it home with her! It wasn't until many months later that I had any idea how important those hundred dollars were to her. For someone who had virtually nothing, that money was literally a godsend.

During the next eight or nine months we chatted on the phone once or twice. In April of the following year Willa attended CLASS, Florence's three-day Christian Leaders and Speakers Seminar. Although she was an attendee at the seminar, Willa, without being asked, helped at the book table when it was busy. I mentioned to her that Florence and I would be back in that area again in June for another large conference in Baltimore. Was there any chance she would be able to come down and help me at the book table once again? Without a moment's hesitation she said, "I would love to."

During the three days at the CLASS seminar, Willa had a chance to tell me she had been reading our books *Freeing Your Mind From Memories That Bind* and its later, companion volume, *The Promise of Healing*.[3] As she read, she realized that some unknown and unresolved issues from her childhood were still seriously affecting her current life, who she was and how she acted. She told me she had suffered from serious depression for most of her life and had remained in a flagrantly abusive marriage for twelve years. Ten years prior to our conversation she had finally pulled herself together enough to flee with her children into the night with only the clothes on their backs!

Willa had learned from reading our books that the Lord Jesus would reveal suppressed trauma if only we would ask Him in prayer. "Is there some time you could pray with me?" she asked me. "I need to know the truth. I need to know if someone did something to me when I was a child." Willa had no knowledge of misdeeds, only large gaps in her childhood memories.

We agreed that the upcoming weekend conference would be an ideal time. Once the function was over we would all be free and could spend whatever time was necessary.

Willa met us for a weekend that would change her life forever!

2

"That Was Jesus, All Right!"

THAT WEEKEND WAS particularly strenuous. The huge crowds responded enthusiastically to Florence's speaking. It seemed there was a continuous crush at the two book tables we had set up. Willa worked at one table with our daughter, and I worked the other. Willa was a tremendous help, and we were gratefully appreciative of her competent assistance. By mid-Sunday afternoon when we finally finished packing up the leftovers, we all had just one thought in mind: crash!

There was just one little problem: two months earlier I had promised Willa I would pray with her once the conference was over so she could learn the truth about her childhood, the truth that might set her free.

Willa had been subject to severe depression most of her life, but the past two years had been what her family called "the great depression." Each day she came home from work exhausted, she told us. At her job she functioned in such high gear she seemed compulsive, and her boss had tried at times to slow her down, fearing she would wear out everybody else. But when she got home she took off her work clothes, slipped into an old comfortable robe and sat on the couch and stared. At times she became almost catatonic, just sitting and rocking. Frequently, her husband from her second marriage had to make supper and serve it to Willa. It was as though she was totally different at home from the person she was at work.

During the great depression, she told us, her overriding thought was, *How can I throw myself in front of one of those big garbage trucks without making the driver feel guilty that he had killed somebody?* She didn't want him to go home to his family every night with her death on his conscience! "If I had been able to figure out how to do it, I would have!" she said.

In Baltimore we packed the unsold books, left the convention center and headed back to our hotel for some well-deserved and much-needed rest. Florence and I were fortunate enough to have a fairly large room including an extended sitting area with a couch and two comfortable chairs. Willa first went to her room to change, pack her suitcase and freshen up while we went to ours. When she was finished she was to come to our room for the promised prayer time. Frankly, I was wishing we could postpone the session until some other time; Florence and I were both so exhausted. Unfortunately, we couldn't because Willa had to drive home that evening so she could be at work at eight o'clock the next morning. There simply was no other option. I forced myself to get ready for Willa's knock on our door; I had to fulfill my commitment to her.

It wasn't long before I heard the expected knock. Willa came in and sat down on the couch; Florence and I took the two chairs. We chatted for several minutes to relax both our minds and our bodies. I then asked Willa a few standard interview questions to help us understand and focus our attention on what the issues might be. Florence, totally exhausted, decided she wasn't really needed and walked over to the bed to lie down and rest. If for any reason we did need her, she would be right there, she said.

Not one of us was prepared for what happened a few moments later. Florence had already dozed off into the first stages of sweet sleep, when one of the questions I asked Willa triggered something that had been deeply repressed. Suddenly she started screaming and flailing the couch. "Leave me alone!" she shrieked. "Get away from me! No, I won't! No, please no, not again!"

At first I didn't understand what was happening. I was sitting on the chair at least six feet away from her, why did she think I was doing something to her? I wasn't even close! Why was she telling me to get away from her?

Willa grabbed the cushions off the back of the couch to protect herself. Decorator pillows started flying around the room! Florence awoke with a start. "What's the matter? What's happening?" She got up and came over immediately to see for herself. "We've got to quiet her down! Someone is apt to call security. What will they think?"

I started to pray in earnest! It quickly became apparent that Willa was not screaming at either of us. It was as if we weren't there at all! We both started calling Willa by name. "Willa, it's all right! You're safe! Willa, can you hear me?"

The ten minutes or so of screaming and flailing seemed to last an eternity before the combination of prayer and calling Willa by name had its effect. Without any warning Willa opened her eyes, blinked, recognized us and asked, "Where am I?"

"You're in our hotel room. You're safe. There's no one else here." Willa was exhausted and collapsed back into the couch. As we ministered to her and reassured her, she started to calm down, and we straightened up the disheveled room.

Then it dawned on me. This was something we had seen only twice before in many years of ministering to hurting people. Willa had been thrown into a spontaneous regression. She had actually relived a traumatic, childhood victimization experience, one that had been completely repressed. It wasn't Willa, the adult woman, but a little six-year-old girl who had relived this horrific event, one that had actually happened but had been completely blocked from her conscious knowledge.

God allows those of us who have suffered such trauma to completely block it from our minds as a coping mechanism. Paul refers to this in 1 Corinthians 10:13.[1] It is often more than we can emotionally handle at the age it occurs. In her book *Repressed Memories,* Arlys Norcross McDonald describes repression as a gift from God because it's His "method of helping us to cope with pain by giving us a temporary numbness."[2]

As Willa settled down and relaxed, she was able to describe to us what she had experienced as a child. It was still fresh in her mind, and now she remembered it vividly. All the details fit, so she knew it was true. She had seen it. She had felt it. She had just been there again as though it had happened that very day. But why had she never seen this tragedy before?

Willa told us that in those ten hysterical minutes she had been back in her great-uncle's small farmhouse where she had lived with her parents, sister and brothers for about three years of her childhood. Her great-uncle, about seventy-five years old, had summoned her into his room and forced her into sexual acts. As Willa reflected on the experience she had just relived, she knew without question this was not a one-time event, nor was this the first time. From her screams and fighting she knew she was old enough to realize that what was happening was ugly, and she didn't want to have to do it again.

It helped Willa to talk about this terrifying memory with us. Gradually all the struggles she had faced in her life began to make sense: the years of depression, the abusive marriage and her prolonged inability to get out of it, the sense that she wasn't worth anything, the compulsive need to prove herself, the suicidal feelings and more. She finally understood.

As frightening and terrifying as the memory was, she felt a sense of release and freedom as she considered it. Now she had an explanation for her years of emotional struggle. It wasn't something wrong with her: she wasn't dumb or stupid; she wasn't a failure. Someone had interfered with God's design for her life. Now there could be hope!

Knowing there was still more work to do and that Willa needed a measure of healing, I asked her, "Willa, would you be willing to go back to that farmhouse now if I promised you that your uncle would not be there and it would be a safe place for you?"

Without any hesitation, Willa replied, "Yes, Fred. I trust you." She simply agreed. She hadn't taken the time to think through the significance of what she was agreeing to.

I asked Willa to thank the Lord in prayer for allowing her to experience and to see the awful trauma. It may seem cold and uncaring to some to immediately thank the Lord for such a tumultuous discovery, but isn't that exactly what God directs us in Scripture to do? "In everything give thanks; for this is God's will for you in Christ Jesus."[3]

Willa did pray and thank her Father in heaven for allowing her to see what had been blocked away in her memory bank for many years. She thanked Him for allowing her to see the truth that was setting her free.

Then I prayed. I also thanked the Lord for allowing Willa to see and to endure what He had permitted her to uncover. I asked the Lord to minister His healing love to her and to do something very special for her. "Lord Jesus, I ask You to fulfill Your promise of John 14:21 for Willa. I ask You to take her back to that farmhouse, but I ask You to remove her uncle so it will be a safe place for her." I continued thanking the Lord, acknowledging that He had all power and authority in heaven and on earth. I closed by simply telling Him that we loved Him, worshiped Him and adored Him. "Thank You, dear Lord Jesus."

Willa's eyes were still closed. I said to her, "Now, Willa, all I want you to do is to answer my questions. Don't try to figure out anything that is happening."

"Willa, where are you?"

"I'm in the kitchen in the farmhouse," she replied promptly.

"Is your great-uncle there?"

"No, he's not."

"I didn't think he would be because I asked Jesus to remove him and to make it a safe place for you." Then I asked, "Is anyone else in the kitchen with you?"

"No, I don't see anyone else."

"Willa, where are you in the kitchen?"

"I'm standing behind the woodstove, hiding. It's the only warm place in the whole house!"

"Willa, I want you to look around the kitchen now and tell me if you see anything else, anything unusual or different." After several seconds' pause with no response, I asked, "Do you see anything, anything at all?"

"No, nothing else, just the kitchen."

This was not the response I was waiting for. I prayed silently, "Lord, where are You? What shall I say to Willa?" Immediately I knew what to say to her next.

"Willa, I want you to look over to your left; look carefully."

After another pause of a few seconds, she said, "All I see is a glow of light."

Silently I said, "Thank You, Jesus!" I knew He was there in that farmhouse kitchen! "Willa, I want you to look at that glow of light. I want you to focus on it. Do you notice anything about it?"

"Yes, I can just barely see the shape of a person there."

A wave of emotion rolled through me. "Good. Keep looking at that figure. What is happening now?"

"It's getting clearer now. There is somebody standing there."

"Can you tell me if it's a man, woman or child?"

"It's a man, and it looks like he's wearing a long white robe!" All of a sudden Willa shouted out, "It's my Jesus!"

Jesus was actually manifesting Himself to the little six-year-old girl in that farmhouse kitchen! Willa was seeing Him in the spirit!

"Willa, can you see His arms?"

"Yes, they're reaching out toward me."

"What does He want you to do?"

"I think He wants me to come to Him."

"Wouldn't you like to go to Him?" Slowly, cautiously, the little girl left her place of safety behind the wood stove and crossed the kitchen to the outstretched arms of the Savior.

During this whole time I was not seeing anything. I was merely relying on Willa's ability to report to me what she was seeing.[4]

"Willa, where are you now?"

"I'm standing in front of Him. He has His hands on my shoulders...He's holding me...He's picking me up and hugging me."

"Does it feel good to be in His arms?"

"Yes, He's so strong, but He's so gentle too."

"Is He saying anything to you?"

There was a pause and then, "I love you, My child," and then, "I will always be with you."

Willa relaxed and allowed herself to be loved in Jesus' arms.

"Is Jesus saying anything else to you?" I asked.

"He's telling me He's sorry...He just put me down, but He's taking my hand. We're walking toward the door."

"Willa, which one of your hands is He holding?" The adult Willa sitting across from me on the couch raised her left hand. I smiled with joy. It was significant. He virtually always takes the child's left hand when He walks with him or her.

"We're outside now. The sun is shining. He's leaving me now. He's walking away from me. He just turned and waved to me. He's going up in the clouds."

"Can you still see Him?"

"Yes, but just barely. He's almost gone."

When He had disappeared from her sight I said to Willa, "You can open your eyes now." Willa looked at me in amazement, but with a calm and contented countenance. "Have you ever seen Jesus before?" I asked her.

"Well, once, kind of, but never like this!"

"Willa, was that really Jesus you saw? Are you absolutely sure?"

"Oh, that was Jesus all right!"

"You told me He had on a long white gown. Did you notice anything else about it?"

"Yes, it was bright white, almost shiny."

"Did you see His face?"

"Oh, yes. I'll never forget it!"

"Was there anything special that you noticed about His face?"

"His face *glowed!* He was so kind and gentle!"

"Willa, do you remember when He walked with you out of the kitchen you told me He was holding your hand?"

"Yes."

"Which hand was He holding?"

"He was holding my left hand."

"Then which of His hands was He holding yours with?"

"He was holding me with His right hand!"

"That's right! You were at the right hand of the Lord, the hand of power and glory and honor!"

"Oh, I never thought of that!"

Reaching for my New Testament, I said to her, "Now I want to show you something even more exciting." I handed it to Willa. "Turn to John 14:19. When you have found it, read it aloud."

Willa read, "After a little while the world will behold Me no more; but you will behold Me; because I live, you shall live also."

"That's good. But now, read it one more time, just up to the line 'because I live.'"

Willa read again, "'After a little while the world will behold Me no more, but you will behold Me; *because I live...*' I saw Him because He lives!" she exclaimed.

"Wait a minute; it gets even better! Drop down to verse 21 and read just the portion highlighted in yellow."

Willa read, "He who loves Me...I will love him, and will disclose Myself to him."

"Does He love You?"

"Oh, yes. He told me so Himself!"

"Did He disclose Himself to you? Some translations say, 'I will...manifest myself to him.'"[5]

"Yes, He did! I saw Him with my own eyes, right there in that kitchen!"

"It gets better! There's one more verse I would like you to look up. Look up Matthew 17:1-2."

Willa thumbed through the Bible until she found it. "Do you

want me to read these, too?" she asked. I nodded.

Willa read, "And six days later Jesus took with Him Peter and James and John his brother, and brought them up to a high mountain by themselves. And He was transfigured before them; and His face shown like the sun, and His garments became as white as light." When she finished Willa looked up at me.

"Willa, how does that compare with the way you saw Jesus?"

"Wow! It was just about exactly the same!"

"Willa, you saw Jesus almost exactly as Peter, James and John saw Him on the Mount of Transfiguration. This means He cares about you. Isn't that exciting? There's just one significant difference. Did you happen to see His hands?"

"No, I don't think so."

"If you had, you would have seen scars on His wrists. You saw Him after the crucifixion. Peter, James and John saw Him before the crucifixion. Otherwise, what you saw was almost identical to what they saw." Willa's eyes lit up.

Then she shared something else that happened in the kitchen. It was something that would have a profound and positive impact on her entire life. It was also going to radically expand the scope of our prayer ministry.

"Fred, when little Willa walked out from behind the woodstove, there were really two little girls who walked out and went over to Jesus. They were dressed exactly the same. When Jesus put His hand on my shoulder, He actually put one hand on the shoulder of each of us. When He did He pulled us together and made the two of us one! Were there two of us?"

The Lord had just revealed to me and to Willa another phase of His miracle healing power. I answered Willa by asking her if she had ever heard the term *multiple personalities*. She said she had. "Well," I continued, "you were apparently what we call a dual personality. Evidently the term multiple doesn't apply to you because there were just two of you, not many little Willas. And Jesus made the two of you one. I think you will begin to see significant changes in your life. You are a new person. You are one now; you are whole. I am certain this change will be be permanent for you. Jesus has done an amazing work in your life!"

We chatted a little while longer about all the Lord had done, and then Willa realized it was getting late and wanted to get started on her drive home. After joyful and tearful farewells, a brand-new Willa headed out the door and home to her husband.

The Lord revealed many facets of His miracle healing power to us, but this was the first time He demonstrated to us how He heals or reunifies fractured personalities. On numerous occasions since then we have seen His glorious, amazing and wonderful healing of people with either dual or multiple personalities. All this through nothing more than prayer and praying His people into His presence! We pray and ask, then He does the work.

A New Willa

The story of Willa did not end when she walked out of our hotel room that Sunday night. About ten days later a sparkling Willa called us in southern California.

"You won't believe what happened when I returned to work," she started. "My boss said to me, 'You're not the same person who left here Friday! What has happened to you?' I told him, 'You gotta believe in miracles!' then went into my office. The next morning he asked the same thing. I said he wouldn't believe me even if I told him.

"On Wednesday morning I was sitting at my desk when my desk intercom rang. It was my boss asking me to come into his office. I took my pencil and pad for dictation. When I entered his office he asked me to shut the door, and I wondered what I had done. To my amazement he said, 'Now! You're not leaving this office until you tell me what happened to you this weekend!'

"He seemed to mean business this time," Willa said. "He really wanted to know. For the next two hours I told him everything. He got more than he bargained for, but he listened to every word. I think he was overwhelmed, but he said that after watching me for the last three days, he had decided I was a different person. I praise God for the work He did in me that

Sunday afternoon. I just want to thank you both again for taking the time to help me."

The healing the Lord Jesus began in Willa's life is continuing. The depression that plagued her for so many years is totally gone. For the first time in her life she was able to lose substantial weight and keep it off.

She is an invaluable member of our ministry team at our Promise of Healing workshops. She is also an exceedingly effective prayer director, assisting others to find similar healing and cleansing from the Lord. Willa assists us regularly at the book table at major functions. In addition to all the Lord has done in her life, she can now add in her head. She is no longer dyslexic! She can quote the total purchase price of several books in an instant to other helpers.

That was just one more part of the total healing the Lord Jesus had done for Willa. She was touched by the Master's hand and experienced the miracle healing power of Jesus.

3

"I Have Seen the Lord"

As MARY MAGDALENE shut the door behind her, the promise of another new day was beginning to peek out over the eastern horizon. The gentle, cool breeze brought refreshment to her confused and downcast spirit as she waited in the darkness by the roadside. Her friends, including Mary and Salome, had agreed to accompany her to the tomb.[1] Her heavy-laden heart was buoyed by the sense of purpose she felt this early morning, but the same questions still whirled through her mind. Why did the chief priests at the temple hate Him so much? Why were they afraid of Him?

Never before had she met such a kind, caring and compassionate man. And now He was dead — they had driven those horrible huge spikes through His wrists and feet. He hung there on that harsh tree in such obvious agony, but He never complained. There was nothing she could do for Him but watch from the distance as if sharing His pain. The soldiers mocked and taunted Him until every bit of life had drained from His body. Mary and her friends had remained on the hillside until it was over, until there was no hope left that He would somehow come down from the cross.

While waiting for her friends, Mary wondered about His very last words, "It is finished."[2] What did He mean? And oh, that darkness and the earthquake! For three hours there was no light. Why in the middle of the day did the sun and all the daylight disappear? That Sabbath night everyone was talking about the huge veil in the temple. Why during that afternoon darkness was it suddenly torn from top to bottom?[3]

Oh, I don't know. I don't understand! I just need to go and be near Him. Salome and Mary should be here by now, she fretted.

Within minutes she saw two figures approaching in the dim early morning. Soon she could distinguish the forms of her friends. "Do you have the spices and perfume?" Salome called.

"Yes, I'm all ready," Mary replied as she greeted each friend with a tender embrace that communicated the grief and sadness they all shared. "Let's go before it gets too light."

It wasn't more than a few minutes' walk to the garden where they had watched on Friday afternoon as Nicodemus and Joseph of Arimathea carefully placed the body of Jesus, wrapped in a clean, new linen cloth, in the tomb.[4] "Who will roll away the stone for us from the entrance of the tomb?" they all wondered.[5] Maybe they could persuade one of the Roman soldiers to do it. Hearts pounding, they walked even faster.

Mary Magdalene was the first one to reach the garden tomb. She was stunned! The stone had already been rolled back and a young man was sitting on it. His face shone like light, and his clothes were as white as snow! The Roman guards had seen him too and were so terrified they seemed frozen in place like dead men.[6]

As her friends caught up to her, the angel of the Lord said to them, "Do not be afraid; for I know that you are looking for Jesus who has been crucified. He is not here, for He has risen, just as He said. Come, see the place where He was lying."[7]

Both fear and joy consumed the three friends — and then questions: How? Who? When? Where was He now? Nothing made sense to them as they tried to understand what they were seeing and what the angel had told them. Where was the Teacher now? How had He risen? Where had they taken Him?

Their awe and amazement were interrupted by the angel. "Go quickly and tell His disciples that He has risen from the dead. He is alive! He's going to go ahead of you into Galilee, and there you will see Him. Tell His brothers, the disciples, what the angel told you. Now go and do as I have told you."[8]

With that the three women turned and ran quickly to tell His disciples what they had seen and what the angel had said. Mary ran to Peter and John, exclaiming, "They have taken the Lord out of the tomb, and we don't know where they have put Him!"[9]

"How can this be? Where were the guards?" Peter asked. Not waiting for an answer, the two men ran to the garden with Mary following close behind. John ran faster and got to the tomb first. There he stopped, stooped at the open entrance and looked in. The linen wrappings were still there. Stunned, he dared not venture inside the tomb.

Peter, always bolder and more aggressive, came up behind John and immediately stepped inside the tomb. He too saw the linen wrappings, and, over to the side, the special face cloth that had been on Jesus' head. It was neatly rolled up all by itself. Emboldened by Peter's boldness, John entered the tomb also. He saw and believed, but he didn't understand. He still had not remembered Jesus' words, "Destroy this temple, and in three days I will raise it up."[10]

Mary stood outside watching the two men. Soon they came out. They said nothing to her. Shock and confusion were on their faces as they turned and slowly walked away, each toward his own home.

Mary, alone now with her grief, stood weeping in the garden. Tears streamed down her face as she stooped and looked inside the tomb. "What have they done with my Lord? Where is He?"

she cried to the empty tomb.

The answer to her questions came quickly. As she peered inside the tomb she saw two young men sitting where the body of Jesus had been lying. One sat where His head had been, and one sat where His feet had been. She was amazed and frightened. Then one of the young men asked her, "Woman, why are you weeping?"

"Because they have taken away my Lord, and I do not know where they have laid Him."[11] Then, Mary heard a voice behind her asking, "Woman, why are you weeping? Whom are you seeking?"

Supposing it to be the gardener, she asked plaintively, "Sir, if you have carried Him away, tell me where you have laid Him, and I will take Him away."[12]

The man responded to her question with just one word, "Mary!"

Instantly recognizing His voice, she turned and cried out with joy, "Rabboni!"[13] Unable to contain her relief and gladness, she dropped to the ground and wrapped her arms around His ankles, as if to keep Him from ever leaving her again.

With tears of praise and worship flowing freely, she could sob only, "Lord! Lord!"

The resurrected Lord Jesus looked down with compassion at the adoring Mary. With the knowledge and wisdom that only He possessed, Jesus said to her, "Mary, do not be afraid. But you must stop clinging to Me, for I have not yet ascended to the Father. Go now to my brothers and tell them I am going up to My Father and your Father and My God and your God. Tell them to leave for Galilee, and there they too will see Me."[14]

"Yes, Lord." With those words the ever-obedient Mary pulled herself together, stood up and went off to do her Lord's bidding.

The words of the Lord comforted her. She was no longer afraid. With a joyful sense of confidence she headed back to town to find the disciples. As she ran, she cried to herself, "Jesus is alive! Jesus is alive! He has risen from the dead just as He said. I have seen Him! I have seen Him! He spoke to me! He called me by my name. He called me 'Mary!' Jesus is alive! I must find the men and tell them. He said they too will see Him! They too will see the risen Lord Jesus. He said so Himself! I can't wait to tell them. They will be rejoicing too when they hear the news. Oh, Jesus is alive! I saw Him with my very own eyes! Oh, thank You, Lord Jesus! Thank You! Now I have hope."

Coming to the first home, she knocked on the door and cried out, "It's Mary! It's Mary! I have news, good news!"

The door opened slowly, cautiously. She was ushered in. The room was dark. There was only a single candle flickering on the small table. She could see six or seven of the disciples sitting on the floor. Several propped their elbows on their knees and held their heads in their hands. Some were crying softly. They looked as if they had been up all night.

What good news could she have? How could she be so joyful on such a terrible morning? "Tell us," one of the disciples asked, "what good news could you possibly have for us?"

"I have seen the Lord!" she exclaimed.[15]

"What? How did you see Him? He is dead! We saw them take His body down from the cross. We saw Joseph and Nicodemus place Him in the new sepulchre. We saw the huge stone rolled into place to seal the tomb. How could you see Him?"

"I did! I did! I just came from the garden. I wrapped my arms around His feet. I didn't want to let Him go! He told me to find you and say to you, 'I am going to My Father and your Father and My God and your God.' He said I was to tell you to leave for Galilee, and there you too will see Him."

Later that evening the disciples, still not sure what to believe, huddled together in a room in Jerusalem. The door was locked. They were hiding, afraid the Jews might come looking for them. There were two short knocks on the door. James answered the door; it was Cleopas and another disciple. They quickly entered the room, and the door was once again securely locked. "The Lord is risen! He has really risen!" Cleopas exclaimed. "Earlier today the two of us were walking on the road to Emmaus. While we were walking, He came up and walked along with us. We didn't recognize Him at all. We were telling Him everything that had happened that weekend. At first He acted like He didn't know anything about it.

"I asked Him, 'Are you the only one visiting Jerusalem who is unaware of the things that have happened here during these past two days?'

"He asked us, 'What things?' We said to Him, 'The things about Jesus the Nazarene, who was a prophet mighty in deed and word in the sight of God and all the people, and whom the chief priests and rulers delivered up to the sentence of death and crucified. But we were hoping that it was He who was going to redeem Israel.[16]

"We told Him what the women had said about being at the tomb early in the morning and not finding His body. I told Him that Peter and John ran to the tomb and found it exactly as the women had said. We still had no idea to whom we were talking. Then He started quoting the Scriptures to us! From Moses and all the prophets, He explained the things concerning Himself. It was amazing! As we approached Emmaus, we asked Him to stay and eat with us, and He agreed to do so. When we sat down to eat, He took bread, blessed it and gave some to us. At that very moment our eyes were opened, and for the first time we recognized Him! It was the Lord! Then all of a sudden He vanished from our sight! He was gone! We got up immediately and came back to Jerusalem to tell you what had happened. The Lord has really risen!"[17]

The others sat there stunned, dumbfounded, not knowing how to react to Cleopas's report. That morning some of them had heard Mary's excited report about seeing Jesus, but they could hardly believe it. Now Cleopas and the other man were saying they had seen Him too. They said they had talked with Him and eaten with Him. How could these things be? How could a man once dead and buried be alive again? How could a dead man talk and eat?

As they were talking among themselves about these incomprehensible encounters, trying to make some sense out of all of it, Jesus Himself suddenly appeared and stood in the midst of them, startling and frightening them. They thought they were seeing a spirit. Knowing their fear and grief, Jesus said to them, "Peace be with you! Why are you troubled, and why do doubts arise in your hearts? See My hands and My feet, that it is I, Myself. Touch Me and see, for a spirit does not have flesh and bones as you see that I have."[18]

They still could not believe what they were seeing and hearing, but at the same time they marveled and rejoiced. Then Jesus asked, "Have you anything here to eat?" They gave Him a piece of broiled fish, and He took it and ate it in their sight.

Then He said to the disciples, "These are My words, which I spoke to you while I was still with you, that all things which are written about Me in the Law of Moses and the Prophets and the Psalms must be fulfilled.

"Thus it is written, that the Christ should suffer and rise again from the dead the third day; and that repentance for forgiveness of sins should be proclaimed in His name to all the nations, beginning from Jerusalem. You are witnesses of these things."

And He led them out as far as Bethany, where He lifted up his hands and blessed them. And while He was blessing them, He disappeared.[19]

Later the apostle Paul would write, "Now I make known to you, brethren, the gospel...that Christ died for our sins...that He was buried, and that He was raised...and that *He appeared*."[20]

And He is yet alive! He is alive today and will appear today to those who love Him and ask Him. He has appeared to me, and He will appear to you. He is our living Lord!

The Bible describes numerous post-resurrection appearances of the Lord Jesus. Three occurred on that first day of the week, the third day following His crucifixion. We have already seen that He appeared first to Mary early in the morning in the garden outside the sepulchre. Later that afternoon He appeared to Cleopas and the other disciple on the road to Emmaus, and that evening He suddenly appeared in the securely locked room in Jerusalem before the frightened disciples.

One week later, He appeared to the disciples again. This time the group included Thomas, who had been missing from the group the previous Sunday evening. You will remember that when the other disciples told Thomas, "We have seen the Lord!" he replied, "Unless I shall see in His hands the imprint of the nails, and put my finger into the place of the nails, and put my hand into His side, I will not believe."

Shortly after Thomas made this comment, Jesus appeared again in the locked room and said directly to Thomas, "Reach here your finger, and see My hands; and reach here your hand, and put it into My side; and be not unbelieving, but believing."

Then Thomas answered and said to Him with words that reverberate around the world to this day, "My Lord and my God!"

Jesus' equally remembered reply was, "Because you have seen Me, have you believed? Blessed are they who did not see, and yet believed."[21]

Jesus manifested Himself again to His disciples early the next morning at the Sea of Tiberias. You may remember that seven of the disciples had gone out fishing at night and caught nothing by morning. When Jesus appeared, although they did not recognize Him, He said to them, "Cast the net on the right-hand side of the boat, and you will find a catch." They caught so many large fish — 153 to be precise — that they could not haul in the net![22]

It is interesting to look at the significance of the word *right* in the Scripture. The right side is always the mark of honor or glory or the sign of power and authority, approval or a pledge.

After His resurrection, the Lord Jesus appeared many times during the next forty days. His last appearance was to the assembled multitude as described in the first chapter of Acts.

In 1 Corinthians 15:8, the apostle Paul relates, "He appeared to me also," a post-ascension manifestation. Paul describes this experience with the risen Lord in Acts 9:3-8; 22:6-11; and 26:12-18.

We have seen clearly that the Lord Jesus appeared in the flesh after His death on several occasions that are recorded in the

Scripture. We also see in 1 Corinthians 15:1-5 that His appearance is the fourth aspect of "the gospel":

"That Christ died for our sins" (v. 3)...

"That He was buried" (v. 4)...

"That He was raised" (v. 4)...

"That He appeared" (vv. 5,6-8)!

Indeed, it is His appearance, an often neglected aspect of the gospel, that comprises the very proof of His resurrection! It is upon this "gospel" that faith, the essential foundation of Christianity, is based. Without the gospel there would be no Christianity, and without Christ's appearances there would be no gospel, for where would be the proof of His resurrection?

4

How Can This Be?

BEFORE I DISCOVERED Jesus' promise in John 14:21, I had never heard anyone mention it or proclaim it. Yet there it is, clear and concise. It is a promise for all time. There is no reason to think it is a promise for only the twelve apostles. It is a promise that you and I can stand on today.

Scripture is clear and plain: "He who loves Me shall be loved by My Father, and I will love him, and *will disclose Myself to him*" (emphasis added).

Other Bible translations use different words to state the same promise:

"I...will manifest myself to him" (KJV).

"I...will...reveal myself to him" (TEV).

"I...will...show (reveal, manifest) Myself to him (AMP).

"I...will...show myself to him" (NIV).

The Greek word used here is *emphanizo*, which may be translated "manifest, known, to make apparent, cause to be seen, to show; to appear, be seen openly"[1] This is so wonderfully clear! Jesus says, "I will show Myself," that is, "I will be seen openly." So why do we hear so little about this beautiful spiritual experience of seeing Jesus in the spirit?[2]

Looking back just two verses to John 14:19, we see that Jesus said to the disciples, "After a little while the world will behold Me no more; but you will behold Me; because I live." Yes, that is why we can behold Him, because we serve a risen Savior, a living Lord. Our God is not dead! He is alive! He will reveal Himself to us if we ask Him! Have you asked Him? He says in James 4:2, "ye have not, because ye ask not" (KJV).

The disciples struggled with Jesus' declaration that they would see Him again, for later in John 16:19, 22 we read:

> Jesus knew that they wished to question Him, and He said to them, "Are you deliberating together about this, that I said, 'A little while, and you will not behold Me, and again a little while, and you will see Me?...you too now have sorrow; but I will see you again, and your heart will rejoice, and no one takes your joy away from you."

Jesus foretold the events following His crucifixion and specifically reiterated to His disciples His *promise* that He would appear to them again following His resurrection. It's clear that this concept was still outside their level of comprehension, for in verse 29, after further explanations, the disciples said to Him: "Now You are speaking plainly, and are not using a figure of speech [a proverb]."

They did not fully understand until after the resurrection, when He appeared numerous times as He had said He would. Is there any reason to think He could not appear today if He chose to do so?

If this concept of actually seeing Jesus in the spirit is in any way troubling to you, why not allow the Spirit of God Himself to speak to you? Let Him reveal to you the truth of Scripture and what He truly means. Let's allow Him to reveal to each of us His purposes and intent in everything He would desire for us to see.

I love Psalms 119:18 for times like these. It says, "Open thou mine eyes [O Lord!], that I may behold wondrous things out of thy law" (KJV).

What other scriptural authority do we have to verify that this phenomenon is true and according to the will of the Father? Below is a list of all the post-resurrection appearances of the Lord Jesus, as recorded in the Scripture. They are divided into two groups — pre-ascension and post-ascension.

Pre-Ascension Appearances

1. To Mary Magdalene "early on the first day of the week" (Mark 16:9).

2. To the "other Mary"...[who] came up and took hold of His feet" (Matt. 28:1,9).

3. To Cleopas and the other disciple on the road to Emmaus. "Jesus Himself approached, and began traveling with them" (Luke 24:15).

4. To "the eleven and those who were with them...He Himself stood in their midst" (Luke 24:33,36).

5. "He appeared to Peter, and then to the Twelve" [no detail given as to time or day] (1 Cor. 15:5, NIV).

6. "Jesus came and stood in their midst, and...The disciples therefore rejoiced when they saw the Lord" (John 20:19,20).

7. "Jesus appeared again to [seven of] his disciples, by the Sea of Tiberias" (John 21:1,2, NIV).

8. "He appeared to more than five hundred brethren at one time" [no time or day given] (1 Cor. 15:6).

9. "Then He appeared to James" (1 Cor. 15:7).

10. To the gathered disciples at the time of His ascension. "And when he had spoken these things, while they beheld, he was taken up; and a cloud received him out of their sight" (Acts 1:4, 6, 9, KJV. See also Luke 24:50-51).

11. "To these [the apostles] He also presented Himself alive, after His suffering, by many convincing proofs, appearing to them over a period of forty days, and speaking of the things concerning the kingdom of God" (Acts 1:3).

Post-Ascension Appearances

12. "And He said [to Paul], 'I am Jesus whom you are persecuting'" (Acts 9:5. See also Acts 22:7-8; 26:14-16; 1 Cor. 15:8).

Other Helpful Scriptures

There are other Scriptures about Jesus that give us helpful information about His appearances.

1. With rare exception, virtually everyone who sees Jesus in the spirit reports seeing Him just as the Scriptures describe Him: "His face shone like the sun, and His garments became as white as light" (Matt. 17:2). "His garments became radiant and exceedingly white" (Mark 9:3). "The appearance of His face became different, and His clothing became white and gleaming" (Luke 9:29).

2. Jesus always chooses the place of His appearing, and often it is a place of special interest or meaning to the individual. For example, He instructed Mary Magdalene, "Take word to My brethren to leave for Galilee, and there they shall see Me" (Matt. 28:10).

3. John describes a similar experience: "Immediately I was in the spirit" (Rev. 4:2).

After studying the passages listed above and after praying men and women into the presence of Jesus, I began to think, *I want to see Him, too.* I regularly asked Him to appear to me. One or two times I thought perhaps I had seen a glimpse or a vision of Jesus, but I was never really sure. I couldn't be certain that I had not simply imagined His presence because I wanted it so much. The sightings seemed like brief snapshots that rapidly came and went. They weren't at all like what others were reporting to me as I prayed with them: clear, describable and alive scenes with Him in which they felt they could touch Him, talk with Him and walk with Him! That was what I wanted.

Finally, one day I asked Florence if she would pray with me so that I too might see the real and living Jesus. I remembered the time a few years before when I had tried to pray on my own to uncover the repressed memories of my childhood victimization. I knew they were there, but I just couldn't see them. Though I had flashes, I never got the memory. I needed to have someone pray with me. When I did, the results were instantaneous.[3] I realized I also needed help to come into His presence. That's why I asked Florence to pray with me. Our prayers that day were different in one salient respect from our prayers with Willa and others. On each of those occasions the person we prayed with had no idea whatsoever what we meant when we asked the Lord Jesus to come to minister to him or her "according to His promise of John 14:21." Therefore, they had no preconceived idea as to what to expect. Their response needed to be completely spontaneous so there would be no question or possibility that we had planted a thought in their minds.

In my case, however, I knew exactly what I was asking the Lord to do for me. I wanted to see Him, and I specifically asked Him to reveal Himself to me. He chose the time and the place; I had no idea where it would be.

First I prayed, and then Florence prayed. "Do you see anything?" she asked.

"Yes. I'm in my parents' bedroom" (on the second floor of the home I lived in for many years as a child).

"Where in the bedroom are you?"

"I'm sitting in a chair between the bed and the door to the bathroom. I know exactly where it is. It's right beside the radiator cover. There's a large window above it." I clearly remembered the large, white dogwood tree that stood outside that window in the backyard. I could see my parents' bed and all the other furniture in the room: my mother's mahogany dressing table ahead of me to the right, then the door to the hall and then her matching dresser on the right side wall. Across the room I could see my father's dresser and, just beyond it, the window between their two closets. In front of my mother's closet, the one on the right, was a chaise lounge and another window just to the right of it.

"How old are you?" Florence asked.

"I'm little." I could see that the chair I was sitting in was a chair upholstered in gold moiré with a rather straight back. I was sitting well back in the chair, and I could see that my feet, with shoes on, went out just a little way over the edge of the chair. "I must be six or seven."

"Do you see anyone else in the room?"

I looked around carefully. I saw the furniture clearly, but no, I didn't think anyone else was there. "No, I don't see anyone else." I could not lie! I could not fabricate His appearance just because I desired so much to actually see Him!

Florence paused, perhaps wondering why I wasn't seeing Jesus. We had thought this would be one of those grand and glorious appearances when He is seen quickly and vividly. I'm sure we both began to speculate about why I wasn't seeing the Savior.

"Look again," she said, continuing, I'm sure, to ask the Lord to come to that room or at least direct us to the place where He would meet me. "Do you see anything different at all, anything you didn't see before?"

I looked around again. My eyes were drawn to the window next to the chaise lounge. "There's a glow just to the left of the chaise."

"Good! Keep looking at it."

"It's Jesus!" I said, with a lump in my throat. "He's standing right there with His arms outstretched to me. He wants me to come to Him."[4]

"Why don't you go ahead and go to Him?" Florence suggested.

I did. I climbed down from the chair and ran around the bed, stretching out my little arms to Him. He picked me up and held me close. I have never before or since experienced such a warm and reassuring hug. I don't remember how long He held me there or how and when He left. I just knew I had met my Saviour. He had answered my prayers and fulfilled to me His precious promise of John 14:21.

I was only six or seven in the place and time Jesus chose to reveal Himself to me. I wasn't even a Christian. I didn't really know Jesus, but He obviously knew me. As a child I had a lot of hurts and often felt unloved. Jesus knew my needs and met them in the bedroom that day. This was not a memory or an experience revisited. It was an appearance in my life at a time and place of His choosing. I was a sixty-four-year-old man asking Jesus to make Himself a reality to me. He chose to appear to a hurting six-year-old little boy. It is a moment I will never forget. I had been touched by the Master.

About two years later during a time of prayer, I felt a desire to see Him again. This time when I saw Him I was an adult at a favorite place in Maine where I had been just four months previously.

> Thomas answered and said to Him, "My Lord and my God!" Jesus said to him, "Because you have seen Me, have you believed? Blessed are they who did not see, and yet believed."[5]

5

Divine Timing

FLORENCE AND I often attend the annual Christian Booksellers Association Convention, familiarly known as CBA. It is the major industry event for all persons throughout the world who are involved in the production and distribution of Christian books, music and other products. CBA is truly an international gathering where each year we see friends we may not have seen since the previous year's convention. It is a time when publishers offer their new releases to bookstore owners and buyers, established authors meet with publishers to talk about new projects, unpublished writers try to interest an editor in the manuscript they have loved and labored over, and foreign publishers come to secure rights to publish editions in their languages and countries.

Those involved in Christian music and merchandising are equally busy doing similar things. There are banquets and breakfasts, teaching seminars and general sessions, all aimed at making the bookstore industry more efficient and effective. For many it is the highlight of their business or ministry year.

On Wednesday night, the fourth night of the convention, Florence and I had no particular dinner plans. We headed out of our hotel to the Marriott Hotel across the street. Having spent many years in the restaurant and food-service-management business, I knew that Marriott began as a restaurant company and still had a high standard for food service. We walked in the door, casually greeted a few acquaintances and headed down the escalator to the restaurant. With such a huge convention in town, restaurants every where were busy, and the Marriott was no exception. We put our name on the list for a "table for two, non-smoking," and headed over to the waiting area, which happened to be the bar, to look for a seat while waiting for our name to be called.

I spotted a couple of empty chairs, and we quickly settled into our seats where we were promptly greeted by a group of booksellers who were sitting next to us. They were waiting, as we were, for seats in the restaurant. After introductions we all swung our chairs around to make a big circle, and soon the booksellers asked if we would like to join them when their table was called. That sounded fine to us, especially since they were farther up the list than we were!

In a short time we were seated in a cozy alcove. Menus were presented, orders were taken, and before long our dinners were served. As might be expected, the conversation soon focused on "What's new?" and "What have you been doing lately?" We told them that God had called us to a ministry of helping hurting people find healing and health in the Lord. Then we mentioned that on numerous occasions we had prayed with people with deep needs who had actually seen the Lord Jesus and who had experienced immediate and somewhat incredible and miraculous healing from being with the Master.

The group at the table was overwhelmed and yet fascinated by what we told them. They asked more and more questions. There was no apparent sense of disbelief but rather a hunger to hear more and more. The reports and testimonies we gave touched on an area of the spiritual realm that was completely foreign to all of them.

They saw us, not as some kind of starry-eyed fanatics, but rather as conservative Christians who were simply sharing with them the amazing and awesome evidence of the power of God at work.

The conversation and the fellowship at the table lasted long after we finished our dinners. I doubt that the waiter got another "turnover" at our table that night because by the time we left, the restaurant had decidedly thinned out.

As we were all getting up from the table and saying our farewells, Michael,* a man who had been sitting at the far end of the table from me, came over to speak to me. I had noticed that he had been listening very intently but hadn't said much.

"I can relate to a lot of the things you've been saying tonight," he said. "I know I was victimized as a child. I've had a lot of struggles in my life. I've been fighting a sense of rejection and anger as long as I can remember. Man, I need what you're talking about. I'd sure love to talk to you sometime."

"I'm fairly free tomorrow, if you'd like," I responded. "I have just one meeting in the afternoon, then I'd be happy to sit down and talk with you."

I quickly offered to help Michael because of a promise I once made to God. He has done so much for me that I told Him I would never turn away anyone who came to me for help. Michael would not be an exception. I hate to see people living in the bondage of rejection, anger, depression or fear when they don't need to, because I know the Lord can set them free.

Michael and I agreed to meet at noon the next day on the convention floor; then we would try to find a quiet, private place where we could talk.

We met and walked around the perimeter of the large convention hall seeking a spot where we could find some privacy. The various hospitality and meeting rooms were all well-occupied, and groups of people filled the halls. I knew if we were going to pray together we needed a quiet place where we wouldn't be interrupted. After several minutes it became obvious there was no such place!

* Not his real name

Finally I spotted a corner where two huge glass windows looked out over the atrium garden. It was about fifty feet from an area where several radio stations had set up tables to conduct author interviews — not very private and certainly quite visible, but at least it was out of the traffic patterns. "Let's find a couple of chairs and pull them over here," I suggested to Michael.

"Looks fine to me," he replied.

We sat down, and Michael began to share with me the areas of struggle in his life. Although he had been raised in a Christian home with a pastor father he said, "I was physically, emotionally, spiritually and sexually abused from early childhood. To complicate the matter, my twin brother and I were 'an accident.' My mother never wanted us, and we both felt rejected the whole time we were growing up. I've been struggling with those feelings of rejection all my life, constantly looking for approval and acceptance. During my teen years particularly, I struggled with my sexual identity. After high school I went to a Bible college, graduated and, following in my father's footsteps, was later ordained. However, I struggled as a pastor and finally self-destructed in the ministry. Next I trained to be a hospital chaplain, but the old nagging fears and pains never went away.

"Through several years of both secular and Christian counseling, I 'got in touch with my past,' as they call it, but it was never put to rest. In fact my anger, another major problem all my life, just became more open. I had learned that it was OK to be angry, so instead of suppressing it as I had always tried to do, I expressed it. I let it all come out as I had been taught. But that didn't solve anything. My anger just began causing me more problems both at home and at work. I was basically forced to leave the hospital and eventually found a job at a Christian bookstore."

I listened to his story and told him, "Michael, I know Jesus wants to heal you and take away all this pain and heartache. I can't do it. In fact, I don't believe any counselor or therapist can do it. Jesus said in Luke 4:18, that He came "to heal the brokenhearted" and to set the captives free (KJV). Your heart has been broken, and basically you're living in bondage to your anger and your feelings of rejection, aren't you?"

"I have been all my life, and I don't want to continue this way any longer," he said. "Plus, it's not fair to my wife and kids."

"You don't have to," I encouraged him. "Jesus can take it all away. He's done it for me, and He's done it for hundreds of others about whom I personally know. And I know He loves you just as much as He loves me. Do you know how I know that?"

"Yes, because He died for me just as He died for you. Fred, I know that intellectually, but emotionally, I've never felt His love!"

What a tragedy, I thought. Here was a man who had probably known the Lord for over forty years but had never known His love or peace with assurance in all that time. He was still striving for it. At least he hadn't given up! I began praying silently, asking the Lord to do something special for Michael that day. I prayed, "Please, Lord, let him know You really love him."

Then I said to Michael, "I think we need to pray and ask the Lord to do something special for you today, something that will take away all the black clouds in your life."

Right there in that very public place, Michael and I, sitting on folding chairs, faced each other to pray. I asked Michael to pray first simply expressing to the Lord his struggles, needs and desires for healing and change. He had no difficulty praying aloud sincerely. No doubt he had spent many hours in the past on his knees, crying out to his heavenly Father.

Then it was my turn. "Lord Jesus," I prayed, "I thank You for Your love for Michael. He knows that You love him, Lord, but he has never really experienced Your love. I ask You, Lord, to come today and minister Your love to him in such a way that he will never again question Your love for him. Lord Jesus, You already know the desire of my heart for Michael, but for his benefit I specifically ask You to fulfill Your promise of John 14:21. I thank You for Your promise that where two or more are gathered together in Your name, there You are in the midst of them. We ask You to come and be with us and be the third member of our meeting together.

"I thank You, Lord, for the power and authority that You have given to us over satan[1] and over all the powers of darkness. I now exercise that power...and, satan, in the name of the Lord Jesus Christ, I take authority over you. I bind you and I rebuke you. I tell you that you are not permitted to interfere in the work of the Lord Jesus Christ in Michael's life today. In the name of the Lord Jesus Christ, I command you to be gone, satan! Be gone from here!

"I thank You now, Lord Jesus, for the assurance we have that satan is gone and cannot interfere. I ask You now, dear Lord, to take Michael to some place that You have chosen to minister Your love to him. I thank You, Lord. I praise You, Lord. I bless You, Lord Jesus. Amen."

With our heads still bowed and our eyes shut, we waited for a few moments. Then I asked, "Michael, do you see anything?"

"Well, yes, I do."

Thank You, Lord, I prayed silently. I knew something was already happening. "Michael, what do you see? Where are you?"

"It's dark, pitch-dark, but I know I'm in my bed. I'm hiding."

"Michael, how old are you?"

"I'm little. I have my jammies on. I'm about six."

"Why are you hiding? What are you afraid of?"

"I'm afraid my father might come in. I don't want him to. I don't like it when he comes into my room!"

Sensing that we might be heading into a memory retrieval and realizing that this was probably not the best time or place for it, I prayed, "Dear Lord Jesus, I ask You to keep everyone out of that room who might try to hurt little Michael; please make it a safe place for him. I ask You to take away his fear, Lord, so that nothing will keep him from receiving whatever You have in store for him." If I had sensed that Michael was being attacked by a spirit of fear, I would have commanded it to leave immediately. But his fear seemed to be not from satan, but the natural fear a child would have if he felt he was in danger.

"Michael, how do you feel now? Are you still afraid?"

"No, not so much since you prayed."

Again I said silently, *Thank You, Lord Jesus.*

"Michael, can you look out from under the covers now?"

"I already am."

Oh, I thought, *that's good.* "Do you notice anything unusual in your room?" I asked.

"No, it's very dark in here. I can't see anything."

"Keep looking, and tell me if you see anything, anything at all."

When praying someone into the presence of Jesus we have to keep the person looking without telling him or her what to look for! (One time I was praying with a young woman who said she was standing as a little girl in a garden. I had asked several times, "Do you see anything, anything at all?"

She continually replied, "No, nothing."

I tried again. "Is there anyone else there in the garden besides you?"

Again she replied, "No, no one."

I knew He must be there somewhere! He had brought her to this garden for a purpose! Again, I asked, "Are you sure there is no one else in the garden? Look again."

With a nonchalance that surprised me she replied, "No, there's no one here, just Jesus."

"Just Jesus! He's the One we're looking for!" He had been there with her all that time. She had no idea He was the One we were looking for!)

Michael was not seeing anything either, until all of a sudden he exclaimed, "There's a bright light outside my window!"

"What kind of a light is it?"

"I can't tell; it's just bright. It's really bright!"

"Can you go over to the window and look at it?"

The little boy climbed down from his bed, walked over to the window and looked out. "It's Jesus! But He's huge. He's so big!"

"Michael, can you tell me what is happening now?"

"I'm outside with Him. He's picking me up. He's holding me, Jesus is holding me! He loves me." I didn't have to say anything more. Michael just went on, basking in the newly discovered love of His Savior.

After a few minutes, Michael opened his eyes. "Fred, I can't tell you what I've just experienced. I was actually with Jesus! He was so big and brilliantly bright. His face shone like the sun. He was standing there with His arms open to embrace me. This is amazing!"

"Michael, while you were with Jesus, did He say anything to you?"

"Oh, yes! I can still hear His voice, it was so kind and gentle. First He said, 'Come to Me, child,' and then, 'I love you; you are precious to Me.' Then He said, 'I formed you; you are Mine.' No one has ever said that to me before. Oh, this is so incredible. I can't wait to call my wife at home tonight and tell her what happened today!"

There was a new radiance in Michael's countenance. I asked him if he remembered that during my prayer, I had asked the Lord Jesus to fulfill His promise of John 14:21. "Yes, I remember you prayed that, but I really can't recall the verse."

"Jesus says in part in that verse, 'He who loves Me...I will...disclose Myself to him.' Did He disclose Himself to you this afternoon?"

"Oh, definitely! He was there. He held me. He talked to me."

"Michael, I want you to think back. Did I at any time ask you to look to see if Jesus was there in that room with you?"

"No, and I had no idea when you prayed and asked Jesus to minister His love to me what you meant or how He was going to do it."

I told Michael, "There's one more Scripture portion I'd like to share with you to show you that what you've just experienced is completely valid scripturally. I wish we had a Bible here. I'd rather show it to you than tell it to you, but you can look it up tonight when you get back to your hotel room. It's Matthew 17:1-2, which says, 'And six days later, Jesus took with Him Peter and James and John his brother, and brought them up to a high mountain by themselves. And He was transfigured before them; and His face shone like the sun, and His garments became as white as light.' Do those two verses describe the way you saw Jesus?"

"Yes, exactly!"

"Michael, you saw the Lord Jesus just as Peter, James and John saw Him on the Mount of Transfiguration, except there was one important difference. Did you happen to see His hands or wrists?"

"Yes, I saw the scars on His wrists when He reached out to me."

"When He was with the three disciples on the Mount of Transfiguration, He had no scars. He had not yet been crucified." I wrote down the two scriptures for Michael so he could look them up later. As we stood to leave, Michael reached over to me and, with tears in his eyes, hugged me with joy and gratitude. He would never be the same. He had been touched by the Master.

A couple of months later I was sitting at my desk in my office when Michael called me from his home. He told me his wife had seen such a tremendous change in his life when he came home from CBA that she wanted it for herself. They were both going to come to the Promise of Healing workshop Florence and I would be hosting the next month.

A year later I met Michael again at CBA. He was truly a new and different man. I mentioned to him that Creation House was considering publishing this book. Four weeks later he sent a letter, excerpted here, to Creation House. After describing his background and how we met, Michael wrote:

> After some completely vulnerable and honest sharing [Fred] led me in prayer to receive healing of the "emotions" or "wounded spirit." During this prayer, Fred, I believe under the direction of the Holy Spirit, led me into healing. As an integral part of my healing I saw Jesus! It is the most holy experience I have ever had. The love and acceptance that I felt cannot be quantified. You have no doubt heard descriptions of how folks have felt God's love flowing as ocean waves into them. That's what I experienced for almost a full hour. All of the old wounds were miraculously cleansed and closed.

From that day on I began to experience, for the first time in my life, the promise of Jesus, "I came to give you life abundantly." My whole life had been dominated by pain and rejection until this healing began. My wife got a new husband. Many parts of our twenty-seven-year marriage have undergone change. The old habits of withdrawing into silence every time I felt rejected are being replaced with an ability to express emotions and communicate openly. There are many areas that we have worked on as I find out who I really am as an adult. The sad little boy no longer controls my reactions.

Yours truly,
Michael[2]

6

No Longer the Least, the Worst and the Last

TRUE TO THEIR promise, Michael and his wife arrived bright and early on the first morning of the Promise of Healing workshop. The always gregarious Michael was in high spirits. Not only was he looking forward to the three-day prayer workshop, but he also was eager to see what the Lord would do for his wife. It had been only three and a half months since his own momentous encounter with the Savior.

Donna,* his wife, was just as eager as Michael. She confirmed the amazing and thrilling changes that had taken place in her husband's formerly angry and discouraged life. This was one happy wife who now was seeking for herself a similar cleansing and healing.

In addition to Florence and me, several other ministry-team members are always present at each workshop. They share their

_____
* Not her real name

own testimonies of trauma and recovery, take part in some of the Scripture teaching, guide and consult during the group and one-on-one prayer times and are also available to minister or meet individually with those needing comfort or seeking answers. After one or two learning experiences, Florence and I made a decision that while the workshop is in session, I do not meet individually with anyone. The whole workshop and much of the teaching falls on my shoulders, and it could disrupt the continuity of the conference if I were detained in a crisis situation outside the meeting room.

I knew that Donna had come to the meeting with both the hope and expectation that I would meet with her privately, as I had done with Michael. That was only natural; whatever he had received she wanted also. She asked me early Monday morning when she could meet with me. I explained our staff policy to her but also assured her I would find a time somehow. Wednesday evening after dinner, when the workshop was over, turned out to be the only time I was available. That was fine with Donna, and I determined to keep my commitment to her.

After our staff dinner following the workshop, I borrowed a car and drove over to the home where Michael and Donna were "housesitting" for the week of the conference. It was already quite late in the evening. The workshop had been spiritually exciting and rewarding but nevertheless physically and emotionally draining, as healing conferences always are. I would have been very content at that hour to return to my hotel room with my wife and just relax and visit, but I had made a commitment.

If we have learned anything in ten years of healing ministry, it is that we should never break a commitment to a person who is suffering from rejection unless it is absolutely imperative to do so. Such a person expects to be rejected again and again. I was not about to be one more contributor to the pile of garbage I presumed Donna was already shouldering.

It was past 9 P.M. before I found the home where Donna and Mike were staying. We had already been together for three days, so there was not much need for time-consuming chitchat.

Donna began to tell me about some of the hurts and confusion she had struggled with throughout her life. Instead of a love for God, she had always felt a dread and fear of Him, expecting Him one day to cut her off from Him. These feelings caused her to believe she was the least, the worst and the last of all. She tended to become panicky at the prospect of any conflicts or trials in her life. "Because of these unshakable feelings of worthlessness, I have strived all my life to find some kind of inner peace that would free me from the constant inner strife that has tormented me," she continued. "I have always felt there was some kind of inner darkness in me from which I would never be released. Because I couldn't deal with looking at myself, I looked at others instead and became very judgmental of any attitude or behavior that I thought was wrong. I have not been much fun to live with or work with."

All of this, I thought, was showing her to be very vulnerable. Michael was sitting there all this time, listening to every word of his wife's outpouring.

It was readily understandable that Donna wanted whatever it was that Michael had gotten. She had a good grasp of what her problems were but still had no knowledge of why she had them. Before we prayed, I asked her one more question that might give us some help in focusing on the source of the dysfunction she was experiencing. "Donna, have you ever felt that there was a hurting little girl inside you?"

"Oh, yes, I know there is!" she replied without thinking of how to answer. That response and the certainty with which she expressed it told me volumes. From past experience I knew the significance of her answer and what to expect from the Lord.

"We could talk about the problems all night," I suggested, "but it's getting late, and I think it's time that we talk to the Lord about the solution." As we prepared to come into the presence of the Lord, I asked Michael to be the silent prayer support for his wife.

As we do with all our counselees, I asked Donna to pray first and told her I would follow her in prayer. I let her know that I would take authority over satan to be sure that he couldn't interfere or block Donna from receiving what the Lord had for her. I prayed, "Lord Jesus, we know You did not create Donna to have to endure all this turmoil in her life. You promised love and joy and peace in the Holy Spirit to each one of us. We do not know Your purposes for Donna tonight, but we do know that You have a perfect plan for her life. We do not ask for memories; we pray only that Your will be done."

In my prayer I also asked the Lord Jesus to fulfill His promise of John 14:21. When I had finished, I simply asked Donna to report to me anything that the Lord was revealing to her.

She promptly reported that she was in the bedroom of a relative's house. She told us she was about four years old, and she was able to say that she was wearing brown high-top, lace-up shoes. She also clearly saw that she was wearing a brown dress her mother had made for her. Her experience was as real as if she were actually back in that bedroom at that very moment. Equally clear was what she saw and experienced next. The relative, a man, orally violated her and then pushed her aside and got up when he was finished with her.

Donna opened her eyes in astonishment. She had never seen such a moment before. As she shared her feelings of what the Lord had chosen to reveal, she was absolutely sure this was true. She knew beyond any doubt that she had not imagined this scene. As she thought about this moment and her life for the past forty-eight years, she said, "I know that wasn't the only time. I just know it, and this makes a lot of sense. Now I can understand all the emotional turmoil I've been through."

Jesus had chosen to give her a memory, a memory that would set her free, even though we had not asked for one.

I knew we could not leave Donna in this released but painful state without asking the Lord Jesus to bring some measure of healing into her life.

"Donna, I think we need to go back to that bedroom. I think there is something more that the Lord has for you. But I think this will be something good and not another painful memory.

Would you be willing to go back to that room if I asked the Lord to remove that man and make it a safe place for you?"

Despite the fact that she was still in mild emotional shock from the revelation, she readily agreed. Once again we prayed. Briefly I reiterated my request that Jesus fulfill His promise of John 14:21.

Instantly Donna was back in that room as the little four-year-old girl. She was sitting in the middle of the floor all by herself, feeling sad, lonely and dirty. There was no one else in the room.

"Donna, I'd like you to look around that room and tell me if you see anything unusual, anything at all that catches your attention."

Within seconds, she replied, "There is somebody standing outside the window."

"Do you recognize that person? Can you tell me who it is?"

"Oh, yes! I can! It's Jesus. He's reaching out His arms to me. He wants me to come to Him." She got up off the floor and ran to Him. Now she was outside with Him. "He's so big!" she exclaimed as she buried herself in His garments. "He's loving me!"

The sad little girl was no longer sad. Suddenly she was reveling in the brilliant white of His tender love. After she had enjoyed a few minutes of this spiritual bliss, I asked, "Donna, where is big Donna?"

"I don't know; she's not here."

"Wouldn't you like her to come over and be with you and Jesus?"

"Yes, that would be OK."

"Would you like to ask her to come over, or would you rather ask Jesus to ask her?"

"I'd rather Jesus asked her."

I encouraged her to ask Jesus to call big Donna.

"Jesus, would You please call big Donna to come over so she can be with us, too?"

"Where's big Donna?" I asked. "Is she coming?"

"Yes, I can see her...She's coming over to us...She's standing right next to Jesus."

58

"Would you like big Donna to hold you and love you too?"

"Would she do that?"

"I think she would if you asked her to."

"Big Donna, would you hold me?" the little voice asked.

"Where are you now?" I asked.

"In her arms. She's holding me."

"Does it feel good to be in her arms?"

"Yes, she's never held me before."

"Would you like to ask Jesus to make the two of you one? Then you would never be apart again."

"OK. Jesus, would You make the two of us one?"

Then there was a pause. The next voice I heard was somewhat different, not that of the little girl. "Fred, this is Donna!"

"Where's little Donna?"

"She just went right inside me. Jesus made us one! He put His arms around the two of us, and we became one!"

Not only had He appeared as He said He would, He had removed the wall of separation and made the two of them into one. Jesus had brought tremendous healing to Donna in that short time. He also reunited the fractured little-girl personality that had been created through repeated victimizations, the hurting little girl inside with the personality of the adult. Now they were one as He had created them.

Donna wrote to me some time later. "The manifestations of my healing were so dramatic and spiritual," she said. She shared the following specific changes that had occurred as a result of the night:

1. I have a new awareness of God's faithfulness in my life from conception till now and [confidence] that it will continue forever. Not only am I comfortable being in His presence, but I find His presence a comfort (1 Thess. 5:24).

2. I can now say with joy that I am the bride of Christ when I walk in confession of sins and His forgiveness. I can say with assurance that I am acceptable to God.

3. The parable of the wheat and the tares in Matthew 13:24-30 used to confuse, frustrate and anger me. How could a loving God allow the tares to grow? Why doesn't He cut them off immediately? I felt that I was one of those tares. I couldn't understand why God let that happen to me or why He allowed me to live. I truly expected God to cut me off and burn me [like the tares were burned]. Now the parable comforts me, and I understand God is long-suffering and patient. Also, the tares that were sown in my life have been rooted up by God's grace, and I am free.

4. I am the head and not the tail (Deut. 28:13). I am no longer the least of all, the last of all who gather in His name. I can accept who I am and what I am, knowing that what He has begun in me He will continue to do until He calls me home or comes for me (Phil 1:6). Trials no longer panic me, for I know He uses them to keep me closer to Him and to see what is in my heart.

5. Strife and striving have ceased. Contentment and inner peace now mark my life.

    "I trust this is all helpful. God bless. Stay warm. Love you both."

                                                            Donna[1]

Today, with individually changed lives and a new marriage relationship, Michael and Donna are actively engaged in giving hope to the many hurting people they meet and in ministering the Savior's healing love to them.

The Rose of Jesus

A beautiful garden unfolded before my eyes. There were green, leafy trees all around me and a large clearing for the light to shine in brightly. The flowers were abundant, flourishing in the lush, green grass. The fragrance of the air was clean, fresh and scented as with perfume.

As I looked around I could see the sky was a deep blue, and there were birds all around singing merrily. My heart was overjoyed at the sights, smells and sounds before me. As a child of about two, I was completely at peace in this haven of rest.

Suddenly I sensed His nearness, and I knew I was in the presence of Jesus! His face and eyes were kind and loving. He was happy to see me! I was happy to see Him! Oh, what joy filled my soul!

As I looked closely at Him, I noticed He was sitting on a swing in the shade of a big tree, swaying gently. Jesus was smiling knowingly. He beckoned me to sit on the grass, and as I did He lifted me onto His lap.

I looked up for a moment, and something lurking in the shadow of the trees caught my eye. There was a little girl just like me hiding there. It was me! But she was wearing filthy, tattered rags. Her feet were dirty, her hair was all straggly and her face was covered in smudges of tears.

I asked Jesus, "How could that be me?" He explained that she is a part of me, the part that holds my shame from what the wicked people made me do.

Jesus beckoned to the little girl to come out from the shadows and come over to us, but she stayed there, her eyes filled with anguish, the same anguish I had felt many times in my life with such intensity. I understood exactly how this little girl was feeling. She couldn't believe Jesus could forgive her for the terribly horrific things she had been forced to do.

Jesus took my left hand as He led me over to the little girl. He squatted down and looked into her face. Jesus touched her tattered clothes, and they became clean and new. He touched her straggly hair, and it became soft and shiny.

He washed away the shame and guilt from her heart; her whole body became clean and fresh. Then He took us out from the shadows and held our heads in His hands. With the same hands that had made me, He put me back together again. Whole and free from the guilt that had plagued me all my life, I was able to look into Jesus' face, unashamed.

While basking in the sheer delight of this beautiful moment, Jesus handed me a rose. He encouraged me to smell the sweet fragrance, touch the soft petals and drink in the beauty of His creation. He said, "This is a picture of you. You are very beautiful."

Now I was a woman, walking beside Him down a garden path. Under our feet was a bed of leaves covering a stone stairway that led down a slight slope under the overhanging trees. There were no shadows anymore, because Jesus is the Light.

I was wondering when all this would end and Jesus would leave me to walk down the path and go on my way. But it continued. I was thrilled to enjoy this sweet communion with my Lord. He turned to me as we strolled along side by side and, with a twinkle in His eye, said to me, "I am the Rose of Sharon, but you are the Rose of Jesus!"

As this delightful scene began to fade from my mind, I noticed something I will never forget. Jesus didn't send me on my way; we continued walking together. I knew from that moment what I know now, that Jesus is always with me. He will never leave me.

The ugly words I had used when thinking about myself were gone; Jesus had replaced them with beautiful words. The picture of a rotten, spoiled and trampled flower had vanished; Jesus had replaced it with the picture of a very rich rose, fragrant, soft and pretty. But it wasn't just an ordinary rose; it was the rose of Jesus.

— Christine, telling her experience of seeing Jesus

7

"Jesus Is Alive, and He Really Loves Me!"

Sarah* is a delightful woman whom I met at a women's conference where Florence spoke. It was through her that we learned an important lesson on being very careful to encourage people who come to us for prayer. As she tells her story in her own words, you'll see how Jesus is sensitive to the needs of the individual.

DEAR FRED, I'M excited to send you this copy of my journal written the day after our first prayer time together. I must say it's exciting to go back and read the detailed account of my prayer time. Upon reading it again, many thoughts went through my head of additional things I would like to note, so I made just a few additional notes in the margins. I had so much I wanted to say, I couldn't type fast enough. I can't tell you how excited I am that you are going to use this as part of your book!

* Not her real name

I was thinking this morning about the other prayer time we had together. That was the time when Jesus took me back to the church I attended as a child and showed me the abuse I had been through when I was three. (This was particularly neat, considering I had no memories before age eight.) During that prayer, after the oral violation had taken place, Jesus cleaned off my face. I remembered that so vividly because it was so miraculous in the way that He cleansed me. First He took His hand and put it on my forehead and then wiped downward. In one wipe He cleaned my whole face. Then I sat in His lap, and as I leaned back toward His chest it was as if I went right through His chest and was surrounded by Him. It's so hard to explain in words exactly what happened. It was kind of like leaning into a big, soft pillow, I became surrounded by Him. I remember feeling so clean and pure.

One additional thing I would like to note is the personal significance of holding Jesus' right hand as we walked over the hills together. I know that after the prayer time I understood what it meant to be at Jesus' right hand, and as noted in my journal, we discussed Scripture relating to being at the right hand of God. But shortly after this prayer time, it became even more apparent to me why Jesus allowed me to hold His right hand.

I have struggled since I was a child with my salvation. I prayed "the prayer" hundreds of times only to still wonder if I was really saved. I rededicated my life many times to the Lord throughout my teenage years but simply didn't understand why I continually questioned my salvation. However, Jesus knew that I fully understood what it meant to be at the right hand of God, and that's why He ministered to me in that way. I know that was His personal way of confirming my salvation for me. I will *never* again *feel* the need to question my salvation. (I know salvation is not based on feelings, but because I felt so dirty and distant from God, I thought I must not be praying genuinely enough to be saved.)

I used to live in actual fear of the second coming. I knew I wanted to be saved and hoped I was. But I was terribly afraid of being left behind. Now, I am anxiously awaiting the return of Jesus. His Word has come alive to me in such a personal way, and I often become teary when Scripture is read. I am constantly amazed by the way God speaks to me through His Scripture and through personal prayer.

Also, I noticed when I read my journal last night that when you originally suggested we pray, I thought prayer was just a formality. Now I have to laugh at that. I have never had such a great prayer life as I do now. Well, actually, because I felt so distant from God, I really didn't have a prayer life at all. I didn't think God really heard my prayers, and I certainly didn't receive *anything* when I read the Scriptures. God has certainly brought me a long way. I am constantly amazed at His love and the healing He has done in my life.

Well, I didn't mean to get so long-winded. Rereading my journal last night brought so much back to my mind that I wanted to share with you. Thank you again for allowing the Lord to use you in such an awesome way. Thank you also for allowing me to be part of your book. I'm very excited and thankful for all the Lord is doing and will continue to do in the future.

Thank you again! I simply can't say enough.

In His love,
Sarah

The following account is an actual entry from Sarah's personal journal:

Well, first of all, this is the first day of the rest of my life. This is my journal, along with daily prayers. Yesterday was the most incredible day of my life! Jesus is alive, and He really loves me!

I went with Lana* and Susie* for a women's conference where the speakers were Fred and Florence Littauer. My intent for the weekend was to find some kind of beginning to a healing

* Not her real name

I desperately needed, but I received much more than I ever expected.

One or two months ago Susie lent me a book called *Freeing Your Mind From Memories That Bind.* Before reading the book, I knew I had been molested when I was about seven or eight years old. My intent for reading the book, however, was actually to help me deal with Mom. We currently have basically no relationship.

After beginning the book I realized it really dealt more with sexual abuse than it did emotional and verbal abuse. And by the time I finished the book, I knew that not only had I been molested, as I had memories of the repeated incidents, but that I apparently had been violated in either an additional way or more extensively than I had originally thought.

I shared with Eric* what the symptoms were. Obviously he was familiar with the areas where I struggled, as he has been a part of my life for eight years and married to me for five of those years. He knew the struggles I had with lack of sexual interest, frigidity in affection, nightmares and unexplained fears.

Almost daily, and sometimes several times a day, I checked all of the closets, under the beds and behind shower curtains for fear that someone was out to get me.

Eric agreed that I had many of the symptoms of sexual abuse, and he was aware of my memories regarding Roger,* who molested me at age eight. However, Eric basically attributed all my problems to my violation by Roger. Listed in the back of *Freeing Your Mind From Memories That Bind* is recommended reading for those who believed, after reading the book, that they had been sexually or severely emotionally abused. Eric and I agreed that we needed to order those books so I could read them and hopefully find some answers about how to begin healing and moving on with my life.

There were ten books to order, along with two specific tapes, and it was recommended that I commit to a ten-week program to read a book a week and do daily Bible study along with a few

* Not his real name

other things. So I ordered the books and started reading a book a week. This was a huge challenge for me because I'm not a big reader and it takes me a while to finish a book. But I believed I needed to commit to reading one a week, and if I applied myself, I could stick with the commitment. I am currently beginning the fifth book, *Your Personality Tree*.

This past weekend I went to the seminar, hoping to be able to talk with Florence about what was happening with the books, my progression and a few questions I needed to have answered to help me continue. Upon arriving at the conference that evening, Susie, who had known Florence since 1979, introduced me to Florence and told her I had been sexually abused and needed to talk with her for a few minutes whenever she might have some time. I was inwardly excited about meeting Florence and was really anxious to be able to talk with her privately. However, after Susie introduced me to her, Florence immediately told me her schedule was so busy she wouldn't have time; instead she would like me to talk to Paula Mitchell, who was also in the ministry and had been sexually abused. I was quite disappointed that I couldn't talk to Florence but figured I'd give Paula a shot. She might be able to help me since Florence didn't have time.

I figured, *Oh well, maybe I'll at least have somebody to talk to who has been through what I had been through.* So we went to Paula and told her what was going on. She talked to me a second or two and basically said I'd need to get back with her tomorrow morning. She didn't know how the schedule was going to go, and she couldn't say exactly what time we might be able to get together.

Well, I'm sure she didn't realize what this response did to me. I felt so rejected that she wouldn't commit a time to me. I wanted to say, "What do you mean, ask you in the morning? I'm asking you now!" But I was so down emotionally and felt so rejected by her answer that I just said OK and walked away. Then I put up my wall, an invisible shield that was obvious to the world, and said, "Stay away! You can't get in, so don't even try. I'm mad at the world, and if I have to suffer, everyone else does, too. You can't cheer me up, so don't even try." I was so rejected, and I knew there was no way I would go back to her the next morning and ask her again; one rejection was enough. If she was too busy for me, I wasn't going to beg. I really thought she didn't care and was just putting me off, hoping I'd go away.

Well, Susie knew something was wrong when I went back to sit with her. I basically told her in jest what had happened and said outwardly, "Oh well, tough. I'm not going to worry about it." So I sat through the program that night, alone and empty.

I felt like no one really cared except Susie, but we had already talked and she couldn't give me the specific answers I needed. She hadn't been through what I had, and I knew she couldn't relate to my feelings. I knew I was emotionally stuck, and if I didn't get help this weekend, I would be stuck for a long time. In Paula's answer I perceived rejection, so I believed I wasn't going to get an answer. I was just stuck.

Well, the program was over, and I had managed to sit through it without cracking a smile, which wasn't hard. During Florence's part, her husband, Fred, came up on stage and talked a few minutes. I remember thinking he seemed nice, and I could kind of relate to him because he reminded me a lot of my dad. I thought I might like to talk to him, but after the previous experience with their staff I sure wasn't about to approach him. So again I said to myself, "Oh well, you're just stuck; quit trying to get somebody to talk to you and just try to forget the whole thing. He certainly is too busy to talk to you."

By this time I really just wanted to be left alone so we could get back to the hotel and I could go to bed. Susie asked me at dinner that night what was going through my mind. Of course I gave some flippant answer and basically sat in silence throughout dinner and the ride back to the hotel.

The next morning we arrived at the conference center and after going to the first small session, met back together in the gym for the large group. About five minutes before it was to begin, Susie asked me again if she could please talk to Paula or

Fred for me. She said she really thought he would talk to me or maybe set up something with Paula for me. I said, "Whatever. I'm not going to beg them, and I don't really think we can get anything accomplished in five minutes anyway. Whatever. I don't care."

Well, Susie went to Fred on my behalf and told him what had happened, explaining how I felt so put off by Paula and really had shut myself down. He told her he would be glad to talk to me. She pointed me out to him, and he came over to me and asked me if I wanted to talk during this session.

Well, we talked about an hour. He asked me a lot of specific questions that were directly related to sexual abuse and specific kinds of abuse. I began to put some things together about my nightmares and fear of being stabbed and fear of the dark and being alone. I learned how so many of my questions were related to one another and actually began to see how some of the puzzle was fitting together. I learned a lot of facts and understood some questions. It was extremely helpful, and I was so appreciative to have had this time together.

I shared with Fred at this time that after reading the books I had finished in the series, I really believed God wanted me to reach out to other people and help them. But I didn't know how. I sure wasn't even close to beginning any kind of significant healing process, and I wasn't about to try to talk to anyone else in an attempt to help them. I didn't even have any answers for my own problems.

After about an hour he asked me if I would like to talk again during the next session. I had a couple of small questions I still wanted to ask him and a couple of ideas I wanted to bounce off him — nothing major, I knew. And I felt a little greedy for wanting to take another hour of his time. But I wasn't about to let go of this source in front of me, so I said yes. We took a break and agreed to come back together in a few minutes when the next session began. So I went and told Susie and Lana I was going to meet with Fred again during the next session, and I would meet back with them for lunch at 12:30.

Fred and I sat down again to continue our conversation. We talked a little about forgiveness, Mom and reactions to other past memories. In our earlier session, through a series of questions, Fred told me he believed there was more to my problems than just my current memory of Roger.

We went over specific questions listed in the book *Promise of Healing,* and based on my answers he explained why he believed I might have been orally violated and threatened by an adult. Needless to say, I was a bit shocked at his conclusion though it did make sense to me.

He said he believed I was threatened, probably with a knife, not to tell, and the threat was probably the source of my phobia of knives, my constant fear that someone was out to get me and my nightmares.

During our second meeting, after about ten to twenty minutes, he asked me if I would like to pray with him. We found a corner, sat behind a divider where we could have a little privacy and started to pray. At first when he suggested we pray together I said, "OK," but I thought, *Well, this is just a formality; it should only last a few minutes. I'll be done soon, then I can take this new information and move forward.* I had no idea what was about to happen.

Fred asked me to bow my head and said he would start us in prayer. He prayed, asking God to be with us and to help me understand and be able to give my problems to Him. After a short prayer Fred asked me to pray out loud and ask the same thing. I didn't want to pray out loud and wasn't quite sure what I needed to ask or how I needed to ask it.

I have been in church all my life and heard thousands upon thousands of people pray, but I suddenly couldn't pray out loud. It just wasn't going to come from my heart, and I wasn't about to just say words, so I told Fred I couldn't pray out loud. He suggested I pray silently. When I was through he would pray again.

We bowed our heads, and he prayed silently as I was supposed to be doing. But I couldn't. I just sat there with my eyes shut for a short time. There were so many thoughts going through my head; I couldn't understand why I couldn't pray. Finally I looked at Fred and said, "I can't pray. I don't even know what to say or how to ask."

So Fred prayed for me. He bound satan and commanded him to leave. He asked me again, but I still couldn't. Then Fred prayed another short prayer. He asked the Lord to take me to a safe place, anywhere at all.

The picture of a lake came to my mind. It was surrounded by green rolling hills. There was a big tree on top of the hill across the lake. I was sitting by the lake looking across it at the tree. I explained this to Fred. He asked me to sit there a few minutes and take it all in, so I did. I leaned back and enjoyed the view.

A short time passed, and Fred asked me what I saw.

I said, "Nothing different. I'm just sitting here." So I sat for a few minutes. Then Fred told me to look around and tell him if I saw anything I hadn't seen before. Was anyone there, or was anything different that I hadn't seen before? At first I didn't know what he meant. There was nothing different. I was still sitting there at the side of the lake. I said, "I don't know what you mean; nothing is different."

Fred said again, "Take a close look. Do you see anything you didn't see before?"

I was thinking, *I don't understand what he means. I've told him what I see.* I knew we had been talking about the abuse that was done to me, and I wondered if I was supposed to see someone who was going to hurt me. I didn't see anything or anyone I hadn't seen before, and quite frankly, I just didn't understand the questions or any point he was trying to make. Nothing was different.

Fred told me to sit there a little longer. So I did. And after a short time, Fred said again, "Anything different at all?"

Just as I started to say no, I realized Jesus Himself had appeared and was standing over me. Jesus? My word! What a moment! I could hardly believe it. Jesus loved me enough to make Himself real to me. I couldn't believe I was seeing Jesus. I didn't know He would come to me that way. But He did. He just stood there and looked down at me. Fred asked me then what I saw, what was happening, who was there. He must have been able to see from my reactions that something was happening. I said, "Jesus!" and cried. Jesus just looked at me for a minute.

Fred asked me what He looked like. I said He was so bright; He just shined so bright. He had on a white robe that just radiated. Then I stood up beside Him, and He held my hand. We stood in silence and looked across the lake. I was in such peace. Jesus said nothing for a while. We just stood together with Him letting me hold His hand. Fred asked me which hand He was holding. I said, "My right."

We stood together for a short time longer, then He lifted me in His arms like a baby. I wrapped my arms around His shoulders and laid my head on His shoulder. I played with His hair, and it was so soft. I just sat there in His arms for such a long time. It was so incredible.

Fred asked me if there was anything I wanted to say or ask Him. I told Him I loved Him. Fred suggested I ask Him to take away my fears, to help me, but I couldn't. I just sat there. I somehow couldn't relinquish my fears; I couldn't ask. I shook my head. I couldn't ask, and I didn't know why I couldn't.

Fred then prayed again, commanding satan to leave, to release his hold and flee in the name of Jesus. I was still at the lake, just sitting in Jesus' arms. He loved me and hugged me and let me sit there as long as I wanted. Fred asked me what was happening again.

I said, "Nothing. He is still holding me."

Fred stated, "You must need a lot of love."

I thought to myself, *Yes, I sure do.* Then as I sat in His arms, Jesus told me He loved me. He told me He would never leave me, no matter what. But most importantly, He wanted me to know He loved me. That's all He said.

It was so incredible to hear Him say He loved me. Me. Just the way I am. He loved me enough to come to me in a way I could understand and feel, just so I would know how much He loved me. He didn't say this to me verbally, but I knew what He meant.

I sat in His arms for a long time. I totally lost all track of time.

Then Fred suggested, "Why don't you ask Him to take away your fears, to help you." I immediately said, "Please Jesus, just help me." I couldn't believe I asked! I now truly believed that Jesus loved me right where I was, no strings attached. He loved me and waited on me. He let me soak up His love and showed me how much He loved me before asking me to trust Him. I continued to sit in His arms for some time. I don't know how long, but in a while we began to walk together over the hills.

Fred again asked me what was happening. I told him we were walking over the hills together hand in hand. Fred asked which hand He was holding. I said, "My left." We walked for a while together, and then He left. I was sitting by the lake, physically alone, but Jesus was in my heart.

He was still with me. I knew He still loved me and was there with me in my heart. His love was all over me. I raised my head and looked at Fred in pure amazement. Jesus had made Himself real to me in the perfect way I needed.

Fred opened the Bible and showed me a scripture. He asked me to read it, but when I read it to myself I became so choked up, I couldn't read it out loud. So Fred read it aloud for me. It was John 14:19, 21:

> After a little while the world will behold Me no more; but you will behold Me; because I live, you shall live also...He who has My commandments and keeps them, he it is who loves Me; and he who loves me shall be loved by My Father, and I will love him, and will disclose Myself to him.

Wow! I just sat and shook my head. Jesus had shown Himself to me. What an incredible revelation!

Then Fred showed me Matthew 17:1-2:

> And six days later Jesus took with Him Peter and James and John his brother, and brought them up to a high mountain by themselves. And He was transfig-

ured before them, and His face shown like the sun, and His garments became as white as light.

Then Revelation 4:2:

Immediately I was in the Spirit; and behold, a throne was standing in heaven, and One sitting on the throne.

My word! I had been in the spirit, just like the Bible talked about. I was so overwhelmed. All I could do was sit there and shake my head. Jesus was really real to me.

Then Fred asked me to recall when I first stood with Jesus by the lake which of His hands I was holding. I said I was holding Jesus' left hand. Then Fred asked, "After you talked with Jesus and you walked over the hills together just before He left, which hand were you holding?"

I said, "His right." And I realized at that exact moment I had walked at the right hand of God. I was so overwhelmed with this that I simply wept. I covered my face with my hands and wept. I was and still am at the right hand of God.

This scripture was real to me. I didn't have to be shown the scripture; I had heard it a million times. And when it became alive to me in that moment, I was overwhelmed. I just sat and cried. Jesus Himself had brought me to His right side. What a miracle! Jesus was with me and in me. I was still in such utter amazement I couldn't believe what had just happened to me. I could only sit and shake my head in amazement. Wow!

After a few minutes Fred asked, in order to make it clear to me, "Did I tell you where to go?"

I said no.

"Did I tell you what to see or think about?"

I said no.

"Did I tell you what Jesus looked like or where to stand or which hand to hold?"

I said no.

He said, "OK, I want to make it clear to you that I didn't prompt you in any way. It was Jesus you saw and Jesus who came to you. I want you to know that."

I said, "Oh, I do! I do!" I was still in utter shock at the fact that Jesus would appear to me that way.

Fred then took me over to the display table and gave me a card with his name and number on it. He told me that my husband or I could call him any time we needed. I thanked him profusely and said, "Fred, I just have to give you a hug." I couldn't stop myself. I loved this man so much for allowing himself to be used by God. He had reached out to me at a crucial time and allowed Jesus in His perfect time to show Himself to me.

Then I walked away from the table and went to find Susie and Lana. I knew we were supposed to meet at 12:30 for lunch. I looked at my watch, and it was 1:30. I couldn't believe it — the whole experience had lasted almost two hours. I went to where we were supposed to meet, and of course they weren't there. I walked back to the gym to see if they had come back there, but they hadn't. So I went outside.

The sun was shining so brightly, and the weather was perfect. I praised God for the beautiful day and the miracle He had brought about in my life. As I walked outside I started to cry at the awesomeness of the experience I had just had.

Then I realized I was still holding the card Fred gave me. As I looked at it, I discovered one side peeled off; something was written beneath the peeled part. When I pulled off the cover, there was the scripture 2 Peter 3:9:

> The Lord is not slow in keeping His promise, as some understand slowness. He is patient with you, not wanting anyone to perish, but everyone to come to repentance (NIV).

The explanation said, "God is patient in His attitude about you. He keeps His promise to save you the moment you turn to Him." I remember feeling that same warmth of unconditional love only Jesus gives. I felt so close to Him because He had given *me* this personal scripture. I started crying again at the second miracle that day. Not only had God promised to take away my pain, but He had confirmed it in writing. What a perfect verse for me. I just couldn't believe what had happened. Jesus is so awesome!

Well, now I really couldn't wait to tell Susie and Lana what had happened. I looked all over for them. I decided to go back to the original place where we were supposed to meet for lunch. Just as I started down the stairs, someone called my name and said something to me. I didn't have my glasses on and couldn't see who it was. I didn't want to admit that I couldn't tell who she was, so I said, "Wait a minute; I can't hear you." I walked over to see who it was, and it was Paula. As I approached her, she told me Susie and Lana had gone to the cafeteria for lunch. They would meet me later.

I felt bad about the earlier misunderstanding on my part toward Paula. I knew she was aware that I had counseled with Fred instead of her, and I didn't want her to feel badly toward me. As I approached her, I started crying and just had to hug her neck. She hugged me real tight and gave me a quick talk about my new tears of joy. She was so sweet and loving. She was truly happy for my new spirit. I didn't really tell her specifically what had happened, but I know it was written all over my face. I knew from her reaction she had no bad feelings at all toward me.

Paula had no idea that I had taken her response badly and said she had actually been looking forward to meeting with me. She said she was sorry she wasn't quick enough to say yes. Consequently, Paula learned a lesson I didn't even know needed to be taught: when asked for help, don't hesitate and don't explain your situation; just say, "Yes, I'll meet with you."

Wow! God had used me to remind someone already in the ministry how to just say yes when asked for help. That meant a lot to me. I knew it was just my perception of her answer that I felt rejected by; most people probably wouldn't have thought much about it. But I guess when you're hurting and you ask someone for help, you need to know the person really cares and is available. It reminds me of the saying, "People don't care how much you know till they know how much you care."

Now it only gets better.

When I counseled with Fred earlier, I told him that while reading my series of books I learned that God wants us to reach out to others and help them in their areas of hurting. I believed that's what I needed to do, but I sure didn't feel I was in a position to help anyone. I hadn't figured out my own situation yet. Yet I kept coming back to this same idea: "Reach out and comfort others as I have comforted you." I told Fred I didn't know how. Maybe in time God would show me who and how.

Fred had also mentioned in passing that there was another young lady at the conference who had come to him and explained that she couldn't sleep the night before. She was awakened during the night and tried to pray for peace and comfort so she could go back to sleep. But she couldn't. She really felt that satan was attacking her and just wouldn't leave her alone.

At the time I didn't think too much about what Fred was telling me about this other woman. After the closing session I went to the display table to get another book. Fred then introduced me to Rhonda,* the woman he had described earlier, and told me she had just experienced the same thing I had. He suggested we get together and talk. So we did, and I realized that God had brought us together. Rhonda had not only had a real encounter with Jesus but also had been shown a memory of abuse that had happened as a child. She had no recollection of this memory until that day. We had only a few minutes to talk, and we didn't get to truly share our entire stories, but God gave me the opportunity to reach out to her.

She was concerned about what her husband would say and how he and others would react. I could tell by her expression that she had a lot of questions about her new knowledge of abuse and about her experience. I just tried to confirm her experience and let her know how God had brought us together. I told her I'd pray for her, and we exchanged phone numbers and addresses. We talked a little more about how she thought her husband would react, and I again tried to listen and say what I could to

* Not her real name

confirm what had happened to her. We said good-bye and promised to keep in touch.

On the way home I wanted to share with Lana and Susie exactly what had happened to me, but I was a little hesitant. I knew they were happy for me and had seen a definite change, but I had to admit that the story might sound a little far-fetched to someone else. But the Lord knew I had to share my experience.

Shortly after our ride home began, the perfect opportunity arose for me to share what had happened. Before I knew it, I was halfway through the story, and I frankly couldn't believe I was telling them all of the details. But they didn't react as I thought they would. They were amazed by what I had experienced, and when I told them of the exact moment Jesus appeared, we all just cried. I shared with them the scripture Fred had shown me, and Susie could hardly read it without crying. We cried all the way home, but I've never had such a joyous cry in my life.

My Prayer to Jesus

Dear Jesus,

Thank You, thank You, thank You. You are so incredibly awesome, words can't explain. You have truly shown Yourself to me in such a real way. I truly know You're Lord. Thank You, Jesus, for saving me, for loving me, for coming to me. I have so much to say, but I know You know my heart. I want to spend so much more time with You, and I can't wait to see what You're going to teach me. You've already taught me so much, but I know You have even more You want to show me.

Thank You, Jesus for loving me so much. Thank You for Your power, Your awesomeness, Your unending love. You're just so incredible.

Jesus, I know You want me to know about my past. I don't understand why I can't remember certain years, but I believe that You will show me in Your perfect time what You want me to know. I am claiming

Your promise to restore my memory. I am claiming Your personal promise to me in 2 Peter 3:9: You are not slow in keeping Your promise, as some understand slowness. You are patient with me, not wanting anyone to perish, but everyone to come to repentance. This is Your promise to me, and I claim it in Your name. You will be faithful. I know that.

Help me to have faith. Help me always to count on You and turn to You. Lord, give me peace; restore me. Help me heal. I truly believe You want me to reach others with Your love. I want to do that. I want to share with others what You've done in my life, so keep me open to what You want to show me at all times. Don't ever let me close up. Thank You, Lord Jesus. Amen.[1]

8

Substantiating Similarities

$\mathcal{O}$SWALD CHAMBERS WROTE, "The questions that matter in life are remarkably few, and they are all answered by the words 'Come unto Me.' Personal contact with Jesus alters everything."[1]

Scripture clearly states that the Lord Jesus has appeared and will continue to appear to those who love Him. This is the most significant verification of seeing Jesus in the spirit. However, there are numerous important and astonishing similarities in the way different people at different times report what they see when they come into His presence. These otherwise inexplicable consistencies are thrilling to behold and are further confirmation of what the Scriptures say.

The encounters with the Master that you have already read about and the others that follow are merely a small sampling of those experienced by numbers of people who have seen the Lord.

It is truly awe-inspiring to comprehend that so many people who had absolutely no idea what they would see or what would happen have, in fact, seen virtually the same thing and in many cases have reported identical experiences. There can be no explanation except that these have been valid spiritual experiences ordained by the Father. Let's take a closer look at some of these similarities.

Jesus' Clothes

Perhaps the first similarity noticed is that virtually every person describes Jesus as wearing a long, bright, white robe. No one, to our knowledge, has ever seen Him in jeans and a T-shirt or in a grey flannel suit or in anything in-between! Some see Him with a sash around His waist; the color of the sash is always gold or a rich blue or purple.

On a few occasions when we asked someone who was just beginning to focus on the image to describe what the person was wearing, he or she has said with some confusion, "Well, it looks like a man, but He seems to be wearing a long dress!"

Once again, it is important to note that when praying with others to see Jesus, we never say, "Do you see Jesus anywhere?" or anything else that would be suggestive. Therefore when His manifestation begins to appear, they truly have no idea what they will see or who it is. Remember Willa's exclamation when suddenly she recognized Him? "It's my Jesus!"

Imagine the emotional and spiritual impact experienced by those who have just visited in the spirit with Jesus and described Him as wearing a bright, white gown and who then look with us at Matthew 17:1-2. Already in a state of awe and amazement, they read this passage: "And six days later Jesus...brought them up to a high mountain by themselves. And He was transfigured before them; and His face shone like the sun, and His garments became as white as light."

Jesus' Transfigured Appearance

"That's exactly the way I saw Him!" they say in astonishment. This is the second significant similarity: After they have visited in the spirit with Jesus, they suddenly realize that His appearance to them was virtually the same as His transfigured appearance to Peter, James and John. They have been privileged to participate in the same realm of spiritual knowledge as were the highly esteemed disciples. If these individuals have struggled with feelings of low self-worth for many years, which is often the case, they are overcome by the realization that they have been welcomed into the veritable and visible presence of the Savior. "Wow! I just sat and shook my head. Jesus had shown Himself to me. What an incredible revelation!" were Sarah's exact words. Sarah is the one who thought, *Well, this prayer is just a formality; it should only last a few minutes. I'll be done soon, then I can take this information and move forward.*

Jesus' Uplifted Arms

A third important similarity occurs shortly after the individuals have seen and identified the One standing, or sometimes sitting, before them. This is the typical dialogue at this point as we ask, "Can you see His arms?"

"Yes, they're reaching out to me."

Once again, virtually without exception, when asked the question about seeing His arms the same answer is always given: "They're reaching out to me." Everyone who sees His arms sees the same thing: the Savior's arms reaching out to all those who are weary and heavy-laden, bidding them to come.

Equally consistent is the reply to our second question, "What does He want you to do?" Invariably the answer is, "He wants me to come to Him." Immediately Matthew 11:28 comes to mind, "Come to Me, all who are weary and heavy-laden, and I will give you rest." He always wants us to come to Him! This was true during Jesus' time on earth as confirmed in the

Scripture. With only seven exceptions[2], everyone who sought the Lord, who needed healing, who needed Him, came to Him.

Why do those who come into His presence in the spirit always see Him with His arms outstretched? Because that's the way He presents Himself and communicates His desire for us to respond. These similarities create more strong corroborating evidence for the reality of the experience.

Jesus' Kind Eyes

As the communicants[3] begin to walk toward Him, the next thing they are apt to notice is His eyes. Often they say, "His eyes are so kind and gentle." Those two words are repeated over and over again. The statement is usually expressed in a comforting and reassuring tone. Jesus does not need to be feared! For some this is a very serious issue. Women who have suffered severe abuse at the hands of men are most apt to fear all men, including Jesus. Those who have been subjected to ritual abuse will immediately see the difference in His eyes from the evil eyes of those who have hurt them. Those who have been reared in love-starved and dysfunctional homes, who expect to be rejected, humiliated and even made to feel hated, will be amazed at His soft and tender eyes. They are eyes unlike any they have ever seen before. Hearing this expression, we are reminded that the Bible frequently describes Jesus as being moved with compassion toward the sick and needy. As we look in the spirit at the kindness and gentleness in the eyes of the living presence of the Lord Jesus Christ, we are comforted with feelings of safety and security.

Jesus' Expressions

Another important similarity is the words Jesus speaks that are heard by those who come into His presence. Very often a lengthy dialogue is carried on with Jesus and is reported line by line to the one ministering in prayer. At the beginning of their visit, the following statements are the ones Jesus is most frequently quoted as saying.

1. "I love you, My child."

Imagine the impact of these words on the one who has never felt loved! Jesus always seems to know exactly the right thing to say! Why should we be surprised? God is all-knowing. God knows every hair on our heads and every desire of our hearts.

2. "You are precious to Me."

These words are heard so often they have to be more than mere wishful thinking on the part of the person who always believed he or she had no worth. Perhaps the strongest confirmation is in the word *precious*. This word is not a part of most people's everyday language. But it is repeated again and again by the Lord Jesus!

3. "Come to Me, child."

These exact words are most often spoken by the Lord when the person is near to Jesus but reluctant, perhaps through fear or uncertainty, to go any closer to Him. He gently encourages him or her by saying, "Come to Me, child." Rarely does He need to say more than that; the person is soon safely in His arms.

Jesus visits with the one who has come to Him for comfort and reassures him or her in specific areas of weakness, insecurity or hurt. He customizes His ministry to each individual's specific needs. Again, why should we be surprised? He may continue talking for some time, but at some point it will be time for Him to depart. Before He goes, He will make the fourth statement so regularly heard.

4. "I'll always be with you" or "I will never leave you."

Both statements say the same thing to the individual and come directly from Matthew 28:20, "I am with you always."

For those who have ever experienced loneliness, these words result in major healing; for others, they are simply comforting.

The individuals who have heard them have been in His presence. They have seen Him. They have been held by Him. They have talked to Him, and He has talked to them. Now He assures them that He will always be available for them, He will never leave them alone. They can call upon Him any time they have a need or desire for Him. He will always be there. Do you have any other friend who can make such a statement and make you feel so absolutely sure it is true?

Jesus says many other things, but at least one of these four statements is heard by virtually everyone who comes into His presence in the spirit. Some have heard all of these statements directly from the mouth of the Redeemer! Once a person has experienced the divine presence of Jesus, he or she is never the same again.

Jesus' Right Hand

After Jesus has spent some time talking, healing and ministering to the person, He may walk with him or her. As we have already seen, He is very likely to take the hand of the child as they walk. Which hand does He hold?

"He's holding my left hand," is the consistent reply (or the left hand is raised). It has been wondrously thrilling to see that He invariably holds the individual's hand in His right hand. He or she is at the right hand of the Lord, a powerfully significant scriptural application. The right hand is the hand of honor and glory, of power and authority!

One time I prayed with an adult woman who, as a child, saw Jesus in the spirit. During the prayer she was a child, and Jesus came into the room to comfort her after some rather nasty business had been revealed to her. He then walked with her out of the room. She was slightly ahead of Him as they walked through the doorway. He was holding her hand.

"Which hand is He holding?" I asked.

She said, "My right."

I was somewhat surprised. Perhaps this was to be the exception. Nevertheless, I asked, "Are you sure?"

"Oh, no," she corrected herself. "He's holding my left hand." I felt reassured.

This, then, is the sixth unique substantiation: we are always at the right hand of the Lord when He takes us by the hand and walks with us.

Jesus' Location

Another remarkable similarity that we have noted is that Jesus never takes two people to the same place! In other words, there is not some specific setting where all people who have been prayed into the presence of Jesus go to see Him. There is not some predictable, mechanical, standardized procedure for taking the one to a certain place to meet the Lord Jesus. On the contrary, the Lord Himself always chooses the place where He will appear. As prayer ministers we never do this. We never suggest a place or tell the individual to try to visualize any place at all. We simply ask the Lord to take the person where He will.

The places He chooses, however, are obviously selected for the meaning they have to that individual. When I prayed with one woman, she said, "I'm on a beach. Oh, I know where this beach is; it's in Hawaii. This is my favorite beach!" As she looked around on that bright, sunny day, there wasn't another soul to be seen. Imagine a premier Hawaiian beach empty, totally devoid of all other human life! But then she saw someone standing near the water's edge some distance from her. He beckoned to her to come! This woman will never forget those moments on her favorite beach, alone with her Savior.

Jesus' Light

Recently I prayed on the telephone with a woman for further healing of scars from her past. I asked her if she saw anything.

"I see the ocean. Oh, I love the ocean!" she exclaimed.

"What else do you see?" I asked.

"I see a hillside and a rock. There's someone sitting on the rock. It must be Jesus!" There's much more to this story, but that will come later. My point is that our telephone prayer occurred in the evening but the hillside setting was in broad daylight. This brings us to our last significant similarity. Jesus always appears in the light. When the locale He has chosen is outdoors, it is always a bright, sunny day! There may be clouds, but they are always pretty, white, puffy clouds. The day is never overcast or dark and gloomy! On some occasions the person with whom we are praying may find himself or herself in a dark place such as a bedroom at night, but when Jesus appears either the whole room is suddenly lit up by His presence or, as Michael exclaimed when he looked outside, "There's a bright light outside my window!" The radiance from the Lord Jesus was so bright that Michael later had no idea if it was day or night outside. All He could see was the pervasive brilliance of the presence of the Lord!

Once again, we should not find this surprising. After all, did not Jesus Himself say, "I am the light of the world: he that followeth me shall not walk in darkness, but shall have the light of life?"[4]

To summarize the substantiating similarities of Jesus' appearances in the spirit:

1. He most often appears in a long, bright, white robe.

2. The person comes to realize Jesus' appearance is virtually the same as His transfigured appearance to Peter, James and John.

3. His arms are outstretched to the one coming to Him, and He beckons the reluctant one to "come to Me."

4. His eyes are "kind and gentle."

5. He often speaks identical words to different individuals who come to Him.

6. When walking with a person, He invariably holds his or her hand in His right hand.

7. The sites He chooses are unique and dissimilar.

8. He always appears in the light.

In the next chapter I've asked my wife, Florence, to tell the story of a special experience she had in prayer with a woman who carried bitterness and guilt over the death of her mother for sixty years.

When I Saw Jesus

Then I was filled with grief. But,
*"In my anguish I cried to the Lord, and
he answered by setting me free" (v. 5).*

Then I was suicidal. But,
*"I will not die but live, and will proclaim
what the Lord has done" (v. 17).*

Then I was weak. But,
"The Lord is my strength and my song" (v. 14).

Then I was in darkness. But,
*"The Lord...has made his light shine upon
us" (v. 27).*

*"You are my God, and I will give you thanks;
you are my God, and I will exalt you" (v. 28).*

— Christine, describing her feelings
about seeing Jesus through
verses from Psalm 118 (NIV)

9

Ruth Came to the Garden Alone

Because Florence and I minister together, I asked her to write about a special experience of ministry she had with a seventy-year-old woman named Ruth.* This beautiful encounter brought immediate healing and long-sought answers and changed Ruth's life forever.[1]

Many of us sing "Because He lives I can face tomorrow," but we have no experiential evidence in our lives that verifies the existence of our risen Lord. For some of us, Jesus is still on the cross or in the tomb. For some Jesus is past tense. Yet when we pray, believing that our Lord is real, and He manifests Himself to us, we know we serve a living Savior. Eyes that have seen Jesus will never see the same again.

Another old hymn proclaims, "He walks with me, and He talks with me, and He tells me I am His own; and the joy we share as we tarry there none other has ever known."

---

* Not her real name

Is it possible to walk and talk with Jesus? Can He tell me things I don't know? Can I experience that joy and peace we sing about? Will Jesus personalize my time with Him and make it special in a way no one else has ever known?

Or are these words just another example of wishful thinking in our eternal search for a rose-garden experience? How can we find the answers?

At the end of the first day of one of our Promise of Healing workshops, Ruth came to me with the question, "How can I know if my mother is in heaven?" Since I didn't know seventy-year-old Ruth or her mother, I had no secret information about her mother's eternal life.

As we sat down on chairs in a corner of the room, Ruth poured out her life story. Her mother had been sickly and died before Ruth was ten years old, before Ruth knew what it was to be a Christian. Her father had been abusive to both the ailing mother and to Ruth when she tried to help her mother. On the day her mother died, her father wouldn't allow Ruth in the room where her mother was, and she spent her life believing that if she could have gotten to her mother's bedside she could have saved her. As an adult she held her father accountable for her mother's death, and she never wanted to forgive him.

Although Ruth became a Christian, she still harbored bitterness toward her father and worried about her mother's salvation. I had no ready answers for her questions, so I suggested we pray and bring these matters to the Lord. Ruth admitted she didn't pray much and didn't know how to begin. I told her I would pray and ask the Lord to show her whatever she needed to see in order to be set free from her bitterness and anger. Then she could tell the Lord whatever was on her heart and ask Him to show her what He wanted her to see.

In praying with someone for healing, we've learned not to tell the person what to look for or give any directive ideas. We put the control into the Lord's hands.

We both prayed, and immediately Ruth found herself standing outside the door of the room where her mother lay dying. She started to cry and said, "I can't go in. He won't let me go in." I prayed and asked the Lord to let her go in to see her mother. She said, "The door is opening. Can I go in?"

"I'm sure you can," I replied.

Ruth reported to me that she got up on her mother's bed and asked her if she was going to die. "Yes, I'm leaving you," her mother said, "but this time you can say good-bye to me."

Ruth burst into tears. "I never said good-bye before," she cried. For several minutes she sobbed and smiled almost at the same time.

Soon she opened her eyes and looked at me. "My mother never held me," she cried out. "All the time I wanted her to pick me up and hug me, but she never did. She was always too sick." We talked about this, and as adults we realized it wasn't the mother's fault; she really was too sick. Ruth prayed spontaneously to forgive her mother for not holding her and for dying. As she finished, I assured her she would feel much better now that she had forgiven her mother.

She then asked, "How can I know if my mother is in heaven?"

I don't have divine wisdom, but I know who does. I suggested we pray again. Ruth asked the Lord to tell her if her mother was with Him. There was no answer, but Ruth saw herself in a garden. She was a little girl, and she was so happy to be out in the sunshine. She described the flowers to me in the detail of a child. "Look at the roses," she said to me. "I love roses. They're like velvet!" She then lifted her head up and asked, "When did you plant this garden, God? I don't remember all these flowers in the backyard."

"Is it a pretty garden?" I asked. Ruth clapped her hands and replied, "It's the prettiest garden I've ever seen. I'm going to take a walk in it and see how far it goes."

Although Ruth's eyes were still shut, she moved her feet up and down and wiggled in the chair like a child. She described the walkway, the trees and each flower as she walked along. We went up hills and down dales as Ruth gleefully described her stroll to me. After what seemed like a long walk, Ruth sat upright and said, "There's someone on the top of that hill."

"Can you tell who it is?" I asked.

"He has on a white robe. Why, it's Jesus!"

"Really? Are you sure?"

"Yes, I'm sure. It's Jesus!"

A look of childlike excitement swept over Ruth's elderly face as the joy of Jesus became real to her for the first time.

"He's calling me. I'm going up to see Jesus!" Suddenly, Ruth stopped. Her hands gripped the arms of the chair and a shocked expression crossed her face.

"There's someone with Him. I think it's my father."

"Your father? Are you sure?"

"Yes, it is my father. He was a very bad man. Why would my father be with Jesus?"

"Ask Jesus," I suggested.

"Will Jesus talk to me?"

"Try it and see."

Ruth asked, "Jesus, why is my father up there with You?"

There was a pause, and then Ruth slumped in the chair.

"What did Jesus say?" I asked.

"He said, 'I have forgiven your father. Don't you think it's time that you did, too?'"

As Ruth sat thinking about forgiveness, I assumed our trip to the hilltop was over, but suddenly she brightened. "There's someone else with Jesus! It's my mother. She is in heaven with Jesus. Thank You, Jesus, thank You for taking care of my mother."

Ruth sobbed again. "She's picking me up. Jesus told her she could hold me tight." Ruth put her arms around herself and hugged herself tightly. "Mama's holding me. Mama loves me. She does; she really loves me." A big smile came across Ruth's face. "Mama really loves me."

After a few moments with her mother, Ruth said, "Jesus is leaving us."

"Where's He going?" I asked.

"He's picking up a stick. He's drawing a circle in the sand. He's drawing a big circle around my father, my mama and me!"

We waited to see what Jesus would do. Soon the circle was completed, and Jesus said, "Now you are a family."

Wow! Jesus not only walks with us and talks with us, but He puts us back together again.

Now you are a family!

Seventy years is a long wait for family unity, but Ruth knows Jesus is real. Jesus put the family together on a hilltop near the garden.

Ruth came to the garden alone while the dew was still on the roses. Jesus walked with her, and He talked with her, and He told her she was His own.

Ruth was touched by the Master, and she'll never be alone again!

10

Now Her Husband Has a Healthy and Happy Wife

I asked Carol Miller, a prayer director on our *Promise of Healing* workshop team, to share in her own words this powerful example of the healing that resulted when a woman we'll call Monica* came face-to-face with Jesus. The encounter occurred during a workshop when I was unable to meet with Monica myself, so I asked Carol if she would meet with her.

What makes this story especially unique is that, although I had previously prayed with and ministered to Carol, she had never ministered to anyone else herself. She had no training or prior learning experience. She had nothing else to draw upon other than her own encounter with the Lord and, of course, the guidance of the Spirit Himself.

Today Carol is a valued member. of our *Promise of Healing* workshop team; the Lord has given her a highly effective prayer ministry with

* Not her real name

96

others. Read on as Carol shares her experience.

$\mathscr{N}$arrived at the gorgeous and spectacular hotel where the women's conference was to be held early on Friday, the first day of the conference. Eager and enthusiastic, I was ready to meet and greet Christian women, as well as kick back and have fun during this special summer seminar at which Florence would be speaking. I knew the Lord had brought all the women there together for a purpose.

It was at this seminar that I met Monica, a lovely lady. She was friendly and had a great smile. Everything about her looked wonderful — marvelous makeup, a fashionable outfit and a cute hairstyle. On the outside she seemed to have it all together, but I soon saw through her facade to the inside where she was falling apart. There was something about her eyes. Behind her smile, there was pain.

When Florence began her Personality Plus presentation, Monica had a feeling that something wasn't at peace within her. She was having a great time, but something was getting in the way. When Florence quoted Psalm 139:1, "O Lord, you have examined my heart and know everything about me,"[1] Monica knew she needed to talk to someone.

She went to Fred first. He spent a few minutes listening to her, then realizing that the schedule made it impossible for him to meet with her for any in-depth time of prayer, he introduced me to Monica. He asked me to talk with her and then to pray with her as the Spirit led me. Me, pray with her? I was stunned! Fred had prayed with me, but I had no training. I didn't know what to do. Apparently Fred had confidence in me. Or was his confidence in the Lord?

We got together on the evening of the second day of the conference. Although she seemed to have it all, Monica was depressed. She was in emotional pain and wondered if life was really worth living. I could relate to those feelings. We talked some more, then I looked at her and asked, "Monica, have you ever felt the love that the Lord Jesus has for you?"

"No. Never," she replied. "I want so much to be able to, but it's like something is blocking that feeling. I'd love to be able to know love, joy and peace, but I never have."

She began to cry, and I suggested we pray. We gave thanks and praise to the Lord, and bound satan from any interference. Then I prayed, "Lord Jesus, please minister to Monica in just the way she needs. Please remove any barriers that may be between her and You, and heal her from her pain."

Within just a few seconds, Monica said excitedly, "I'm three years old, and I'm in the upstairs hallway."

"What are you wearing, Monica?"

"I'm wearing a pretty, ruffled dress. I even have on my Mary Jane shoes."

"Are you alone?" I asked.

Her voice changed from excitement to fear. "No, my grandfather is here. He wants me to go with him into the bathroom. I don't want to go, but he's making me."

The grandfather took her into the bathroom and closed the door. It was there that her grandfather horribly violated her. When he finished, he left the room. Little three-year-old Monica just sat on the bathroom floor, crying and trying to hide.

She had forgotten the incident until now, but her emotions had not forgotten. Monica was sobbing as she relived the awful abuse she had endured long ago. She was feeling with great intensity all the hurt and shame the abuse had caused her. She wept until she had no more tears to shed. Then Monica opened her eyes.

"It was awful," she said. "How could he ever have done that to me?"

"Monica, let's pray that the Lord will take you back to where you were," I said. "You've seen the memory. Now there's healing to be done."

"I don't want to go back there again!" she stated. "I don't want to go through that again."

"Monica, let's ask the Lord to make that room a safe place for you to be. Let's come to Him and ask Him to bring you healing."

I prayed that the Lord would make that room safe for Monica. We prayed her into the presence of the Lord, and He quickly brought her back to that bathroom.

"Where are you, Monica?" I asked.

"I'm back in the bathroom," she replied.

"Are you alone?"

"I think so, but I'm not sure."

"Look around and tell me if you're alone."

"I'm not alone! There's someone behind the shower curtain!" Monica exclaimed. Though she didn't know who was behind the curtain, Monica wasn't afraid.

"Who is there with you?"

"It's Jesus! He came out from behind the shower curtain! Now He's lifting me up in His arms!"

Monica's voice was filled with excitement and wonder.

"He's telling me it's OK now," she said. "He's patting my back and cleaning up my dress. It's a white dress now; before, it was blue. It's white and really pretty again."

"I am cleansing you. I am washing you whiter than snow," Jesus said to her. "You need not feel ashamed. I know everything about you. I have always been near to you, as I am now. You need never be afraid again. I have healed you of this awful pain."

"Jesus, why did this happen?"

"I give everyone free will, Monica, even your grandfather," Jesus said. "This experience was meant for harm in your life, but I will turn it to good for you. You will now be able to listen to and comfort others who have endured much the same. You can tell them there is hope. You will be healed, and I will be glorified."

"Thank You, Jesus. I love You, Jesus," Monica cried in gratitude.

"Remember, I am always here with you, Monica. I love you!" Jesus said.

Monica opened her eyes and looked at me. Oh, those eyes!

They were so different from the eyes I had seen before. They were big and bright, no longer clouded by that hidden pain.

"It's a miracle! I saw Jesus, and He held me and healed me!" she exclaimed.

From that moment on, Monica became the very special person God had created her to be. She went back to the conference, and her friends just couldn't get over the difference they saw in her. They were so excited and asked her what had happened. Without hesitation and with great joy, she gave testimony to the healing Jesus had done in her!

She left the conference and flew back home. When she departed from the plane, she ran to the loving arms of her husband. He saw in her a happiness he had never seen before. He knew he had a healthy, happy wife and was eager to hear what had happened to her to cause such a wonderful change.

Her dynamic, moving testimony has inspired many persons to seek healing. Her husband has sought the Lord's help and healing for himself; and he has encouraged others as well.

When I think of Monica and others like her, a scripture comes to mind: "He welcomed them and spoke to them about the kingdom of God, and healed those who needed healing" (Luke 9:11, NIV).

Monica now understands that the One who created her (Gen. 1:7-23) and the One who raised Lazarus from the dead (John 11:1-44) is the same One who held her in His arms and healed her. We serve a living Lord. He is the One who was, the One who is and the One who is to come![2]

11

What Wonders He Has Wrought

The wonders our Lord Jesus works never cease to be awesome and amazing. One of these awesome wonders is the way He uses people and their experiences to bring His comfort to others.

The Lord heals in many ways, and one of those ways is through those who are willing to make themselves available to Him. One such person is Paula Mitchell. A staff member of both our CLASS seminars and Promise of Healing workshops, Paula has become a gifted servant of the Lord in bringing many into His healing presence since her own "reunion," as she describes it. Because Paula was the vessel the Lord Jesus used to bring His healing to Mona* and Robert,** I have asked Paula to relate these two episodes in her own words.

As with all of our true illustrations, only the

* Not her real name
** Not his real name

101

*names and places have been changed to protect
the privacy of those who have granted permission
to tell their stories.*

Before June 22, 1993, I thought the Lord Jesus was finished doing miracles. I read about them in the Bible. I told those miracle stories to my children and grandchildren. I believed all of them, but I believed they happened to others. Since that day — my reunion day — I have seen many miracles. Jesus is in the miracle business today, just as He was all those years ago. Mona, a woman I prayed with, was given a miracle by the Lord Jesus.

On the first day of a three-day CLASS seminar, Mona could hardly stand and say her name. Tears welled up in her eyes each time I even looked at her. I prayed for her that evening and asked the Lord to show me how to help her. As I walked into the room on the second day, Mona approached me and asked if I would have time to spend with her that day. "Yes, of course" was my immediate answer. Then I whispered, "Thank You, Lord."

Mona was so ill at ease that we talked about the weather for about five minutes. Then I asked her one of the questions I had asked myself so many times, "What are you afraid of?"

"That you will think I'm an awful person."

"Mona, don't worry. As I have told my children, there is very little I have not either tried or been caught at myself."

"Well," she continued timidly, "I have never told anyone, but I had an abortion years ago."

"How do you feel about the abortion now?" I asked.

"Awful! I can't look at the children I had years later without thinking that I am a fake. How can I consider myself a mother when I killed one of my children? I believed the people who told me it was just a simple medical procedure. If that is the case, then why can't I get it out of my mind? Why can't I get on with my life?"

With that admission, Mona broke down in tears, heart-wrenching tears that only a grief-stricken mother can cry.

"Was it a boy or a girl?" I asked.

"I don't know; I try not to think about it. Only God knows."

"Why don't we ask God then?"

"He would never help me after the terrible thing I did," Mona said sadly, but then she decided tentatively to reach for this new hope. "Could we ask Him? Really?"

Mona and I found a small room and started what was to be the beginning of her healing journey.

"Dear Lord, we come to You today as two women in search of healing. You promised to heal the brokenhearted. I lift Mona up to You. Only You, Father God, know what she needs. I ask You, dear Jesus, to minister to her as only You can. I ask that You put Your balm about her that she may cease to hurt."

"Dear Jesus," Mona prayed, "I need to know that You love me. Please forgive me for the abortion. I need to know where that child is today. Help me, O God!" Mona's eyes remained shut while I continued to pray silently. I watched Mona for a moment or two as she sat there quietly.

"What's going on, Mona?" I asked. I noticed her body beginning to relax and a newfound peace came over her face.

"He's over there playing ball with a man."

"Who's over there?"

"A boy, oh, it's my son. He's almost ten years old, and he's playing ball with...oh, it can't be. It really is! He's playing ball with Jesus!"

"Jesus?" I questioned.

"Yes! And now Jesus is coming over here," Mona said with fear in her voice. "I can't let Him see me. I don't deserve to be near Him."

"Don't be afraid. He won't hurt you."

"He wants me to sit with Him!"

"What is He saying to you?"

"He loves me; He loves me! I am a good mom!" Tears began to flow as Mona continued.

Suddenly Mona knew his name! "I love you, Michael. I know

that you understand, even if I didn't know why I aborted you. Yes, you can stay with Jesus. He'll take care of you. Yes, we will be together again."

"Thank You, Jesus, for letting me meet my son. You have cared for him so well."

"Is there anything you want to give to Jesus?" I asked Mona.

"Yes, I want Him to take my shame, but what if He won't take it?" she replied.

"You can give it to Him. It's OK. Just hold it out, and it will be gone," I tried to reassure her.

I asked if she was still holding onto the shame.

"No!" she responded elatedly. "Jesus took it and said I was never to think about shame again, only to think about my son who is with Him."

After a few more moments of silence, I asked, "What is happening?"

"Jesus and Michael are walking away. But Jesus said anytime I wanted to I could come to visit."

As she opened her eyes, Mona threw her arms around me and hugged me tightly. "I can go home tonight and not cry after I say prayers with my children. I can go to my husband as a pure woman and not a dirty one. Jesus took all my shame, dirtiness and guilt away. Thank you, Paula."

I replied, "I did nothing but pray. Jesus, your Savior, did it all!"

Robert's Story

After a Promise of Healing workshop, a friend asked me if I would pray with a man named Robert. I was tired because I had also spoken at church that evening. But I knew if I did not pray with Robert, I would probably feel guilty all the way home. I remembered how a tired Fred prayed with me after a grueling weekend. Could I do less?

Robert had struggled all his life with rejection and worry. His dad died when Robert was quite young. He remembers, "Dad was my hero, but I never knew if he was a Christian." Oh, how he longed to know that answer.

I asked Robert the question I so often ask, "Have you ever felt that there was a hurting little boy inside?"

"Yes. And I even know why he cries," Robert replied.

"Let's pray and ask the Lord the question that has haunted you all these years." I suggested.

"Dear heavenly Father," Robert began, "You know the sadness I carry with me. Where is my daddy now?"

Robert began to cry in the sobs of a heartbroken little boy.

"What's going on?" I asked Robert.

"It's the coffin. My daddy's in the coffin."

Robert stopped crying and sat upright. His face changed completely.

"What's up?" I asked.

"I have to be a brave boy. Mama will be upset if I cry," he said.

"Is your mama there?"

"No, just me. I'm only five years old, but I can't stand being alone here with Daddy. I just hurt so much." With that Robert again broke into tears.

"No one is going to hurt you," I reassured him. "It's OK to cry. You can let the hurt out."

"My name is Bobby. I am little. I miss my daddy." Robert sobbed.

Suddenly Bobby began to smile.

"What's up?" I asked once again, knowing from his body language and facial expressions that something was going on.

"Look. Look. Look!" cried Bobby. "It's Jesus."

Since I had asked the Lord Jesus to minister to Robert as only He could, I was not surprised Bobby could see and hear his Lord.

"What do you want to ask Him?" I cautiously asked.

"Lord Jesus, where is my daddy?" the voice of little Bobby asked. "Is my daddy with You, Jesus? Is he in heaven with You?"

"What is the Lord's answer?" I asked.

"Yes! Yes, my daddy is standing right next to Jesus. He's

there. Oh, the coffin is empty. Daddy is a Christian!"

Tears flowed freely from Robert's eyes.

"Jesus and Daddy are holding my hands. I want big Robert to be here. We both missed Daddy so much. Robert needs to be here. Jesus, can Robert be here too?...He can, oh goodie. Big Robert, please come with Daddy, Jesus and me. It's OK to cry here."

"Who is with Jesus now?" I quietly asked.

"We are all here. Jesus is talking with us. We're just loving Daddy and Jesus. Jesus says He will always be with us. He won't leave us like Daddy had to," said a very self-assured Robert.

"Is there anything else you would like to ask Jesus?" I said.

Robert sat still for a few minutes then in a firm, strong voice said, "Jesus, will You make me whole. Help me to embrace that hurt little boy. Make us one."

"Thank You, Lord Jesus. Thank You for loving me enough to give me my heart's desire."

When he opened his eyes I asked Robert what happened.

"I can grieve now. I can cry not only the sad tears, but tears of joy at knowing my dad is with the Lord. I am whole, there is no longer a hurting little boy inside. Jesus hugged us together. I am whole, really whole!"

As we ended the evening with a prayer of thanksgiving, I also thanked the Lord Jesus for giving me the wisdom to say yes to prayer. In my own strength I would not have been able to sustain prayer for one hour. I thought of the disciples who did not rely on Jesus' strength and fell asleep outside the garden when He asked them to pray. Without the strength of the Lord's hand I would not be able to pray with those in need.

Jesus has healed me, Mona, Robert and many more. The Lord Jesus Christ is still in the miracle business. Yesterday, today and tomorrow!

12

Guidelines for Praying Someone Into His Presence

HOW DOES It work? How does it happen? What do we have to do to make it happen?"

When people ask me how to go about praying someone into the Lord's presence, my answers to all three of the questions posed above are surprisingly similar and frankly uninformative!

How does it work? I really don't know.

How does it happen? I don't know that, either.

What do we have to do make it happen? Nothing except pray!

We do not have any authority over the time, the place or the certainty of Jesus' appearances in the spirit. They are totally, completely and only within the scope of His sovereignty. Isaiah 9:6 (NIV) says, "The government will be on his shoulders." In this case, that means it is up to Him.

There is nothing we can to do to make it happen except to ask and to pray. He has already promised that He will manifest

Himself to those who love Him.[1] Therefore, we simply need to ask Him to fulfill His promise, and He does so in His own time.

On those occasions when He is not seen, it is not necessarily the case that He is not there or has chosen not to "appear." It may mean that there is an obstruction or a veil that prevents the one looking for Him from seeing Him. Reasons for this veil or "blockage" will be discussed in the next chapter. On the other hand, since disclosing Himself in the spirit is totally His prerogative, within His jurisdiction and no one else's, there may be reasons why He waits or even withholds His disclosure, which only He understands.

Prayer is perhaps the least understood and, for many, the least practiced aspect of living life "in Christ." I am continually grateful that He has not ceased to teach me more about prayer, its power and its application. Since my initial experience of praying another person into His presence, I have learned a great deal. In this chapter I will share with you some of the concepts He has taught me, that you, in turn, may receive the joy that comes from praying someone into His healing presence.

Many believers have seen Him on their own — that is, without having someone else pray with them. For most of us, it seems far more effective to have a friend or loved one pray with us. I prayed "on my own" for some time without ever really seeing Him or coming into His presence. The day Florence prayed with me, I was in a place that He chose, and I saw Him almost immediately. The only explanation I can give for why it is best to have a prayer partner is found in Matthew 18:20, "Where two or three are gathered together in my name, there am I in the midst of them" (KJV).

Think on that verse for a moment. Our Lord Jesus says that when two or more believers meet together to pray, to worship or to fellowship *in His name,* He is already there — in the midst of them. Since He is already with us, perhaps it is only a matter of opening our spiritual eyes so we may actually see Him. The key phrase in the verse seems to be that we gather "in His name." Then we are meeting together for spiritual purposes as distinguished from personal, social or other human purposes.

When praying with another to come into Jesus' divine but incarnate presence, the most important thing to remember is never to make a suggestive comment or question to help the other person see. Failure to follow this basic recommendation may mean you are planting thoughts or images in the person's mind. As a result, any manifestation that follows will be subject to the question, "Did I really see Him, or did I think I saw Him because I was told to look for Him?" Confusion is one of satan's tactics, and he always tries to steal the blessings God bestows. It is most important — in fact it is essential — that any appearance be entirely spontaneous and only the work of the Lord. He does not need our help. He needs only for us to come to Him. He says that we should ask and He will do the rest. He is the only One who can do it!

To preserve spontaneity, it is best if the persons with whom you are praying have no idea whatsoever that you are going to ask Jesus to appear to them. Clearly, it might be more effective if they didn't read this book until afterward! However, it is God who is sovereign and determines the results. With those who ask you to pray with them that they too might see Jesus, as I did with Florence, it is necessary for you to remind them not to imagine anything or try to visualize anything in their minds that they are not actually experiencing. That would serve no valid purpose. They would be deceiving themselves.

In planning your prayer together, select a time devoid of stress, pressure and any other kinds of constraints. Set aside at least an hour and protect the prayer time from all interruptions: telephone, children, doorbells or other plans. It may also be helpful to reduce the light in the room and to be sure that no bright lights are shining in the communicant's eyes. For some people, such light may be an interference.

What are some valid reasons for setting up a time for such prayer? Any or all of the following:

1. The person has some needs or issues that have resisted resolution, and he or she would benefit by bringing them to the visible Lord.

2. He or she needs to experience the unfailing and unconditional love of the Lord and to feel the warmth and security of being held in His arms.

3. If the person has had difficulty in accepting the reality of the existence of a living God, seeing Him would put an end to that question forever.

4. The person may acknowledge a hurting little girl (or boy) inside, a dual personality that needs to be brought to the Lord for reunion, or oneness. (In professional counseling this is often referred to as an inner child.)

5. Your friend has a deep-seated anger problem and earnestly wants the Lord to cleanse it.

6. The growth of faith and trust seems to have been limited, a situation that could be obliterated by seeing Jesus in the spirit.

7. You have been praying, and the Lord has spoken to you directly or the Spirit has prompted you to pray your friend into His presence for the work that He wishes to do in that person's life.

8. Your friend has specifically asked you to pray him or her into the Lord's presence because he or she wants to see Jesus and possess every spiritual inheritance available to God's children.

What is a valid reason for *not* setting up such a time of prayer? When one of you has heard or read that it is possible to see Jesus in the spirit and you just want to see if it really works! We must come as children unto the Father. We do not come to question His authority or promises or to sit in any form of judgment on His wondrous works. The Lord Jesus Himself in Luke 4:12 (quoting Deut. 6:16) said, "Do not put the Lord your God to the test."

Interestingly, neither your faith nor your prayer partner's faith seems to be of significance in asking Jesus to disclose Himself.

You are simply asking Him to fulfill His promise to us that He will manifest Himself. When you pray with someone and he or she suddenly cries out with surprise and amazement, "I see Jesus!" your own faith will leap forward and upward! You too will rejoice! You will cry out in your heart, "Thank You, Jesus!" for the Lord has used you to bring this blessing of His appearance to your friend. Since you will have asked Him to appear, you will also know with certainty that God does indeed hear and answer your prayers.

Suggestions for Praying Others Into His Presence

While it's true that all you have to do is ask Jesus to manifest Himself, I offer some suggestions here for those who need them to get started. These are steps that have proven most effective in my experience.

Help the communicant to focus spiritually.

As the two of you sit down to talk and pray, immediately focus his or her attention and mind on Scripture, on the Lord and on the spiritual and emotional needs in his or her life. This is not the time to focus on material needs; you are preparing for spiritual blessings and healing of emotional issues. It is best not to start your conversation centered on the everyday things of life: the children, "What's new?" the job, the church, hobbies or sports.

To put your friend at ease, assure him or her of the compassion and healing power of the Lord, and point out that He understands all our needs and desires, and, in fact, already knows them before we even express them. Share some comforting and assuring scriptures such as:

> "I know the plans that I have for you," declares the Lord..."You will seek me and find me when you seek me with all your heart. I will be found by you...and will bring you back from captivity" (Jer. 29:11,13-14, NIV).

He hath sent me to heal the brokenhearted (Luke 4:18, KJV). (Note that this verse does not proclaim He will change our circumstances but that He will bring spiritual or emotional healing.)

Come unto Me, all ye that labour and are heavy laden, and I will give you rest (Matt. 11:28).

These are just a few suggestions for scripture to use. Be prepared with verses that are familiar and have been of special meaning or comfort to you. Assure your friend that you know the Lord Jesus is alive, has power, cares for him or her and will meet his or her needs! So what is there to fear or to be anxious about?

You may suggest, "I believe the Lord wants to do something very special in your life today," or "I believe the Lord wants to show you today how much He loves you." Suggest whatever the Holy Spirit leads you to say. When you sense it is time to pray, tell your friend, "Let's pray together now."

It is always helpful, but not essential, to have a third person present as a *silent* prayer supporter. This person can also serve to verify later what you or the communicant might have said. It is not at all unusual for the prayer supporter to receive a blessing as spiritually impacting as the one who actually comes into His presence.

Encourage the communicant to pray aloud.

Let the communicant pray first, however brief or uncertain the prayer may be. In doing so, he or she is obeying the Lord's directive and offer to: "Come unto Me." If he or she is fearful or unsure of how to pray, make some simple suggestions. It is important that this prayer be said aloud so you, as the prayer partner, can share in this time of communion in the spirit.

Sometimes people say at this point, "I can't pray," or "I don't know how to pray." It may be necessary to lead these hesitant ones in prayer by saying phrases as if they were speaking and

asking them to repeat the same words after you. Continue leading them phrase by phrase until the prayer is completed. In this
way they are actually praying aloud, and you are interceding for
them. The Spirit will guide you as you pray, and after the amen
you might ask, "Did that prayer express the desire of your
heart?" You will be delighted at the number of times the friend
you are praying with will respond, "Yes, exactly!"

The exact words or length of the prayer is not of great importance. It is important that the other person does pray, even
briefly. Remember the Lord does not need to hear our prayers;
He already knows our desires and petitions before we ask.[2] But
He does want us to ask! He does want us to come to Him.

Pray on behalf of the communicant.

Now come to the Lord on behalf of your friend. It is good to
begin with praise and thanksgiving. At some point in your audible prayer, ask the Lord to fulfill His promise of John 14:21.
(Don't say what the promise is.) That is all you need to ask Him
to do. He already knows the desire of your heart. You could ask
silently, but then your friend would not hear your request and
would not know what you have prayed for. In my own experience, I have never yet met anyone who knew what John 14:21
was when I asked Jesus to fulfill the promise in it ("He who
loves Me...I will love him, and will disclose Myself to him"). It
is important that the communicant not know it in order to maintain spontaneity and to prevent him or her from trying to
visualize or see something that is supposed to be there or that he
or she wants to see. Later, after the Lord Jesus has appeared in
the spirit, when you share that verse with the individual, he or
she can excitedly authenticate the experience.

Your prayer need not be lengthy. Remember the Lord's admonition, "Woe to you, scribes and Pharisees, hypocrites...for a
pretense you make long prayers."[3]

Bind and banish satan so he cannot interfere.

This step is essential for three profound reasons. First, you do not want satan to interfere, and frankly, he will know very quickly what you are up to and try to do everything he can to create an obstruction that will lead to failure. There is no reason to allow him this opportunity. Since you already have full authority and power over him,[4] it makes no sense not to exercise this power.

Second, it will comfort your friend and give him or her a sense of spiritual security to know that you have sensibly taken this precaution.

Third, when your time of prayer is over, the person will remember that you bound satan and realize that everything he or she saw or experienced had to be from the Lord. Because the enemy was first banished, the experience could not have been from satan.

Here is a suggested prayer to bind and banish satan. It is to be spoken audibly and with authority. It should not be loud or shouted, for the volume of your voice is not what brings about compliance but the authority of Jesus' name. The prayer, or command, to satan could even be whispered and be equally effective!

> In the name of the Lord Jesus Christ, I take authority over you, satan. I bind you, I rebuke you, and I banish you in the name of the Lord Jesus Christ. I tell you, you are not permitted to interfere. I command you to leave, satan. In the name of the Lord Jesus Christ, be gone! Be gone from here!

The exact words of your command to satan are not significant. The important thing is to speak with authority as Jesus did when He spoke in the Scriptures to satan, demons or evil spirits. He always spoke with authority. You do the same. He has already given that authority to you. The only eight words in the commandment above that are essential are "in the name of the Lord Jesus Christ!" By ourselves we have no power whatsoever over satan or his emissaries. They will, in fact, laugh at us in scorn. But when you invoke the name of Jesus, they immediately know you mean business!

If you are familiar and experienced with taking authority over satan, use your own words of command in prayer. If you are not, then the words above will do an adequate job for you. Do not forget to use them! Do not forget to exercise your God-given power and authority.

I would like to be able to tell you that once he is bound and banished, satan will leave you alone, knowing his presence is not desired. Unfortunately, he is not a gentleman and does not play by the rules. He is thoroughly evil and serves no purposes but his own, one of which is to destroy or render Christians immobile and ineffective. Another purpose is to control all aspects of the spiritual and material realms. Therefore you will need to be alert continually to recognize any interference or any blockage that he tries to throw into the middle of your prayer proceedings. You may need to throw him out again, "In the name of the Lord Jesus Christ!" Do so immediately, without any hesitation and with the authority that has already been given to you. If there is one thing he does understand and knows he must obey, it is the authority in and of the name of the Lord Jesus Christ. I'll share additional insights on this important issue in chapter 18.

To prepare your friend for what will happen next, as you conclude your own prayer you might say to the Lord, "Now, Lord, I ask You to take [person's name] to the place You have chosen for [him or her] and come and minister Your healing love to [him or her]. Thank You, Lord Jesus. Now we wait upon You. Amen."

Coming Into His Presence

From this point on, you do nothing more than ask questions. Ask only about what your friend is seeing, hearing or experiencing. In order to preserve the integrity of the experience, it is essential that you never ask or say anything which could be described as leading the person to give the type of response you are hoping to hear!

During this period continue in silent prayer and communion

with your Father in heaven, but keep your eyes open. The communicant, however, must keep his or her eyes closed, otherwise he or she will be seeing in the flesh and not in the spirit. With your eyes open, you will be able to observe any changes in expression as the Lord takes your friend through the experience and you will be able to ask the appropriate questions, such as "Is something happening now?"

Your dialogue might sound something like this:

"Mary, do you see anything?"

"No, not really. Am I supposed to?"

"You might. Just let me know."

"I think I see a mountain."

"That's good. Keep looking at it, and tell me anything else you see."

"Now I can see it more clearly. It's a big grassy hill."

"Is it daytime or nighttime?" (Note: This is asked in a way that is not suggestive.)

"It's daytime. The sun is shining, and I see some bright clouds."

"What else do you see?"

"I see big trees on the hill, and I see a brook at the bottom of it."

"Look around. Do you see anyone there?"

"I think so. It looks like someone is standing by the brook."

"Mary, where are you?"

"I'm near the bottom of the hill, sitting near the brook."

"How old are you? Can you tell me?"

"I'm little, about six."

"What are you wearing? Can you tell me?"

"Yes, I have on a dress."

"What color is it? Can you tell?"

"Yes, it's yellow and has white ruffles." (Note: Any such positive identification that your communicant can give you helps to solidify the details of the time and place.)

"Oh, that sounds pretty. Look at the person you saw by the brook. Is it a man, woman or child?"

"It looks like a man, but it looks like he's wearing a robe!"

"That's good. Can you tell me what color it is?"

"Yes, it's white. It's bright white!"

"Mary, do you know who that is? Do you recognize him?"

"Yes, I think it's Jesus!"

"I think it is, too. Where is He standing in relation to where you are?"

"He's on the same side of the brook, but right near it."

"Do you see anyone else around?"

"No, just the two of us."

"Can you see His arms?"

"Yes, they're reaching out to me."

"What does He want you to do?"

"I think He wants me to come to Him!"

"Why don't you to do that? Do you think you can walk over to Him?"

"Yes."

"Are you walking over to Him?" (Note: Since we are not present at the scene, we must rely on what Mary reports to us.)

"Yes, I'm right in front of Him now."

"Can you see His hands?"

"Yes, He has scars. Somebody's hurt Him."

"What is He doing now?"

"He's picking me up. He's holding me in His arms! Oh, it feels so good. He's so strong, I feel so safe. Nobody's ever loved me like this before! Oh, I don't ever want to leave!"

"Is He saying anything to You?"

"He just said, 'I love you, My child.' Jesus said He loves me. I never knew He really loved me before! Oh, Jesus, I love You, too! Please don't ever leave me! He just said, 'I will always be here for you, whenever you need me.'"

"What's happening now?"

"He just put me down. Now we're walking together by the brook. He's holding my hand."

"Mary, which hand is He holding?"

"He's holding my left hand." (You allow Mary to walk by the

brook with Jesus, but at some point you will know it is time to ask another question.)

"Is anything else happening?"

"Yes, He just told me it's time for Him to leave me for a while, but He will be back any time I need Him. He's walking away from me, along the brook. He just turned around and smiled at me!"

"Can you still see Him?"

"Just barely....now I don't see Him anymore."

"Mary, you can open your eyes now."

Now it is time to review with Mary what she has actually seen and experienced and to confirm it in her conscious mind lest the enemy try to steal it away from her. Invariably he will try.

Confirming His Appearance

The first thing you might ask is, "Mary, did you actually see Jesus?" Let her answer in her own words each time, as you continue validating her response with comments and questions such as:

"Are you sure it was Jesus?"

"Have you ever seen Jesus before today?"

"Did I at any time ask you to look for Jesus?"

"I never even mentioned His name until you told me it was Him, did I?"

"How do you feel now about Jesus' love for you?"

"He talked with you, and then He took you for a walk, didn't He?

"Have you ever seen that hillside and brook before? Is it like any place you have ever visited in your life?"

All of this serves to confirm to Mary that this was uniquely her experience with the Lord Jesus and that you did nothing to orchestrate it. Next you are ready to show Mary the really exciting part.

"Mary, do you remember that in my prayer I asked Jesus to fulfill His promise of John 14:21?"

"Well, yes, I do remember you said that."

"Do you know what John 14:21 says?"

"No, I really couldn't say. I'm not that good at reciting scripture."

"Let's look in the Bible and see what it actually says. Here, you look up John 14, verse 21, in my Bible, and as soon as you find it, read it aloud." After Mary reads the verse, focus on the key phrase for today, "He that loveth me...I will love him, and will manifest myself to him" (KJV). Mary, the word *manifest* may also be translated as *disclose,* or *reveal.* Did Jesus reveal Himself to you today? Did He appear to you?"

"Oh, absolutely. Nobody could ever tell me differently. He was there. He held me in His arms. He loved me!"

"Mary, there's one more thing I'd like you to think about. Do you remember when Jesus started to walk with you along the brook and you said He was holding your hand? I asked you which hand He was holding. Do you remember what you said?"

"Yes, I said He was holding my left hand."

"That's right. That's what you said. If He was holding your *left* hand, which of His hands was He holding yours with?"

"He was holding me with His right hand."

"Exactly! That means you were at the right hand of the Lord, the right hand of God, the right hand of honor and glory, of power and authority. Mary, you were at the right hand of the Lord Jesus!"

"Oh, I never thought of that, but yes, I was. Wow! I must be important to Him!"

"Yes, Mary, you are very important to Him. But wait; there is something else I want you to see in the Scripture. Turn to Matthew chapter 17, and when you find it read verses 1 and 2."

> And after six days Jesus taketh Peter, James, and John his brother, and bringeth them up into an high mountain apart, and was transfigured before them: and his face did shine as the sun, and his raiment was white as the light" (KJV).

"How does that compare with the way you saw Jesus?"

"It's the same. It was just about the same. His robe was a bright, bright white, and His face glowed just like it says. Oh, this is incredible! This is so exciting!"

"Mary, there is just one significant difference in the way you saw Jesus from the way in which the three disciples saw Him. What was it?"

"The scars?"

"Exactly! When the three of them saw Jesus, He had not yet been crucified, so there were no scars. Otherwise, you saw Him in virtually the same way!"

After a few more minutes of ministry to Mary if you sense that it is time to conclude your session, you might suggest, "Mary, why don't we take a few moments and thank the Lord Jesus for what He has just done for you?" Once again, encourage your friend to lead the prayer of thanksgiving.

Your friend's life will never be the same again. It is unlikely that he or she will ever again wonder, *Does Jesus really love me?* Your friend will know He does, because he or she has been with Him, in His divine presence.

13

Blockages to Seeing Jesus in the Spirit

ABOUT A YEAR or so ago, some good friends visited our home overnight. Stan* and his wife, Barbara,** had called a few weeks in advance to say they would be in San Diego for a conference and would love to stop in for a visit. Our continuing friendship began several years earlier when Florence and I spoke at the conservative, evangelical church where Stan had pastored for many years. We were thrilled at the chance to see them again. We are home very infrequently due to our travel and ministry schedule, so we were delighted that our available days coincided.

As we sat around the dinner table that night, the conversation soon centered, as it so often does when Christians fellowship, on the works the Lord had been doing in our lives. We told Stan and

* Not his real name
** Not her real name

Barbara of the awesome and wondrous changes we had seen God bring about in people's lives when they came into the living presence of the Lord Jesus.

"Come into the presence of the Lord?" they asked. "To actually see Him in the spirit?" This was completely outside their spiritual or experiential reference points.

Neither of them had any knowledge of this part of our ministry, so we had to give them a full report including some of the miraculous occurrences. They knew our ministry included teaching and the books on the four personalities. Our conference in their church had had a profound positive impact on their congregation. They also were aware that we were ministering to hurting people through prayer, and they knew about the Promise of Healing workshops, but what we were sharing with them that night seemed to fascinate them, and yet it seemed foreign to anything they had heard before. They kept asking questions and wanting to know more. They didn't shut down and try to change the subject as some might do. They were genuinely interested.

As the dessert dishes were being cleared, Stan asked me, "Would it be possible for you to pray with me to see Jesus? I've never experienced anything like this in my whole life, and I would love to have the opportunity. I don't want to miss any spiritual blessing the Lord has for me."

I assured my friend I would love to do so. How can we resist when a dear friend asks us to be a part of their receiving one of God's gifts?

After a little more conversation, the women left us to go into the kitchen to clean up. Normally I'm the chairman of that detail, but that night I thought we'd better get to Stan's request. We explained to our wives what we planned and went into my little study. Shutting the door and dimming the lights, I briefly confirmed to Stan that we would do nothing more than pray and leave the rest up to the Lord. I gave him just the most basic and brief instructions as to how we would proceed.

As far as I know, Stan, as a man of God, is as much without spot or blemish as any man can be; he has wholeheartedly and sacrificially served the Lord throughout his entire life. He is a man for whom I have always had the highest respect and admiration.

Stan prayed first, sincerely and simply expressing his prayer in the beautiful, rich, bass voice the Lord has given him to enhance his preaching. Following Stan's prayer I came before the Lord in my usual manner. After a pause of a few seconds, I asked, "Stan, do you see anything?"

"No, not yet," he answered.

"Just keep watching. I think soon the Lord will reveal something to you...Do you see anything now?"

"No, not really."

Lord, I prayed silently. *I thank You for already knowing Stan's desire and mine as well. I ask You now to come and reveal Yourself to him in whatever manner You choose.*

Still there was silence from Stan. He wasn't seeing anything. All he could perceive was a gray blankness. At one point he thought, with some uncertainty, that he saw a small light in the grayness. I rebuked and banished satan again to be sure he was not interfering. Still there was nothing.

We cannot fabricate or orchestrate what is not there. Stan was not seeing anything at all! After about half an hour I suggested to Stan that he open his eyes. We had had a quiet half-hour communion before the Lord, and that should not be negated. However, Stan never saw Jesus in the spirit. We turned on the lights and returned, with some disappointment, to our wives.

Oswald Chambers wrote, "Why does not God reveal Himself to me? He cannot...as long as you won't abandon absolutely to Him...If a man cannot get through to God it is because there is a secret thing he does not intend to give up."[1]

It was some time later that the Lord seemed to show me why Stan's prayer had not been answered that evening. I perceived that Stan's heart and his head may not have been connected that night. In his heart he really did want to experience this blessing, but intellectually the whole idea was too far outside the perimeter of his doctrinal boundaries — his spiritual comfort zone.

There may also have been some skepticism and a desire to see "if this would work."

The distance from the head to the heart may be described as life's most difficult span to bridge. This is especially true in the spiritual realm. There are two ways this difficulty may manifest itself. First, in our heads, intellectually, we may believe, accept and agree. It makes sense. Yet in our hearts, our emotional reference points, the concept may be totally beyond what we feel the Lord Jesus would do for us or what we would dare ask Him to do.

Second, the reverse may also occur. In our hearts, we desperately desire something to be true, to be real; it would make much of life so much easier. Yet when we think logically, rationally and intellectually, it makes no sense whatsoever. The concept of seeing Jesus in the spirit thrusts some believers directly into this conflict, which may be attributed to doctrinal postures.

This inner conflict is expressed in these opposing statements:

"*Yes*, I see what the Scripture says. I would like it to mean what it says." (My heart believes it.)

"*No*, no matter what the words say, that is too radical. I simply cannot conceive that it could be true." (My head cannot fathom it.)

This is why we have suggested repeatedly that the person with whom you are praying have no prior knowledge of what you will be asking the Lord to do. For some people the ability to see Jesus in the spirit is simply not something they are ready to intellectually or emotionally accept as reality. Perhaps it would have been better for my friend Stan if we had never discussed it. On the other hand, we probably never would have had that particular time of prayer together without our dinner table conversation.

Once a person has been in Jesus' presence, however, that difficult span between the head and the heart has already been effectively bridged. The gulf no longer exists!

The other reason already discussed for not disclosing the objective during this time of prayer is the joy of spontaneity! Jesus' presence becomes a delightful but totally unexpected blessing.

A Blockage Broken

I was reminded of this blessing of spontaneity and of another type of blockage recently when I shared an amazing telephone prayer time with Jill.* I had seen Jill only a few weeks before at a retreat at which both Florence and I had spoken. Jill reminded me then that she had been to a Promise of Healing workshop three years earlier, and she told me how much it had helped her. "I have been in therapy ever since, and I'm doing well, but I still feel as though there are some unresolved issues in my life."

I responded by telling her that the Lord had taught us many new things since the workshop she had attended three years ago. I told her I'd love to hear about her journey and share with her the new steps we had learned. I knew she probably had never seen Jesus, and I wanted to be sure she had that opportunity. The retreat weekend was so busy we were never really able to get together again, but we arranged a later time to pray together on the telephone. I, of course, said nothing that would give Jill a clue as to what I intended to ask Jesus to do for her except that we would pray for some additional healing. We both prayed, expressing our desires to the Lord Jesus, and I asked Jesus to fulfill His promise of John 14:21 (which did not alert Jill to anything special because she was not familiar with the verse). Then I bound and banished satan. After our prayers, I asked Jill, whose eyes were still closed, "Do you see anything?"

"No," she replied after a moment or two, "everything's blank." I waited and asked again. Still nothing except she said, "It's just black; all I see now is black."

I recognized the blackness as a probable sign of demonic interference, so once again I exercised my God-given authority over satan and commanded him to leave. Immediately the blackness disappeared, Jill said, but there was still nothing but blank. We waited as I continued to pray silently, but still there was nothing. Then the Lord led me to ask, "Jill, have you ever felt as though there was a hurting little girl inside you?"

* Not her real name

"Oh, yes, I know there is!" was her instant reply.

"Have you ever talked to that little girl?"

"No," she answered thoughtfully, "I don't really think so."

"Does she have a name?"

I was somewhat surprised by Jill's prompt and certain answer. "Yes, it's Helene."

"Do you think I could talk to Helene?"

"Well, I don't really know."

"Would you ask her? Just ask her if she would be willing to talk to your friend Fred."

Jill must have asked her silently, for in a moment I heard a somewhat different voice, younger and sounding angry, answer, "What?"

"Are you Helene?" I asked.

"Yes."

I spent the next minute or two getting acquainted with, befriending and reassuring this little girl who had never met me before. I was a total stranger to her. Then I asked, "How old are you, Helene?"

"I'm six."

"Helene, I would like to pray with you. Would that be all right?" Helene, feeling more comfortable with me now, gave her assent, and I prayed. Jill's eyes were still closed, but now I was talking to little Helene.

"Helene, do you see anything?"

Immediately Helene answered, "Yes, I'm standing at the door to the barn." Later I leaned from Jill that she had been raised on a farm.

It wasn't long before Helene was able to report to me that she was climbing up the ladder to the hayloft. There the Lord revealed to her some things that should never have happened to a little girl. When the hayloft was empty except for little Helene sitting there, I asked, "Helene, do you see anyone else there in the hayloft with you?"

"No," she answered. I asked her to keep looking around because I had made a special request in my prayer, and I felt certain the Lord had heard me. But still Helene could see no one.

Then I asked, "Helene, is there anyone behind you?" Sometimes you can just sense when someone is standing behind you.

"Well, I think there might be," she answered.

"Can you turn around and look?"

"Yes, there's a man sitting there against the wall."

In my heart I said, *Thank You, Jesus!* I knew it must be Him! "Helene, can you tell me what He's wearing?"

"Yes, it looks like He has on a white robe."

"Do you know who that man is?"

"It's Jesus, I think."

I knew it was, for little Helene had identified Him herself. "Helene, can you see His arms?"

"Yes, they're reaching out to me."

"What does He want you to do?"

"He wants me to come to Him, but I don't think I can. I'm too dirty."

After a little encouragement and reassurance that Jesus really did want her to come over to Him in that hayloft, Helene continued reporting the events of her experience to me as I listened on the other end of the telephone. Next she got up and haltingly walked over to Jesus. She was reluctant for Jesus to hold her because she felt so dirty, so I suggested that she ask Jesus to make her clean. She did ask, and in a moment Helene indicated she was standing there in a clean dress. Then she allowed Jesus to hold her in His arms. She felt so safe with Him.

After she had enjoyed several minutes of Jesus' comforting love, I asked her, "Don't you think we ought to ask Jill to come over and be with Jesus, too?"

Now that she was clean, Helene felt comfortable with that idea, and at my suggestion she asked Jesus to bring Jill over also.

"Is big Jill there now?" I asked.

"Yes, she's right here with us. She came when Jesus called her."

"Would you like Jill to hold you, too?"

Helene seemed to think about it for a moment, then she said yes. I encouraged her to ask Jill to hold her, and in a second or two she was able to tell me that Jesus had handed her over to Jill, who was now holding her. When she was comfortable in Jill's arms, I asked, "Would you like Jesus to make the two of you one?"

Helene thought for a moment and then asked, "Jesus, would You make us one?"

"What has happened?" I asked. The next voice I heard was Jill's!

"She's gone," Jill replied.

"Where did she go?" I asked, careful not to plant any answers in her mind.

"She just went inside me!" Now Jill and Jesus were together in that hayloft, and after Jesus ministered His love to Jill for several minutes He departed, promising that He would never leave her.

Afterward Jill told me how free she felt. She no longer had to function as two personalities. It takes additional energy to be two people. The changes in Jill were complete and permanent.

The blockage Jill experienced was broken when the Lord prompted me to ask about a hurting little girl inside. To this day I don't understand why Jill had a blockage. I do know that the Lord taught me something new and very significant that day. In addition, Jill experienced a powerful and marvelous work of the Lord in her life. She was touched by the Master.

Of all the people with whom we have prayed to see Jesus in the spirit, I would say fully nine out of ten, or about 90 percent, were actually able to see Him the very first time they prayed. But what about the other 10 percent? Why is there some blockage that keeps them from receiving this portion of their rightful spiritual inheritance? Over the past years we have come upon a number of explanations that reveal some possible sources of interference. These possible blockages are listed below, in no particular order, to help you understand why some of the people with whom you pray may have no success at all while others come immediately and clearly into His visible presence.

1. Putting God to the test

This may have been what our pastor friend Stan was unwittingly doing. We always need to come to the Lord as little children, ready and willing to receive whatever He chooses to give us with no sense of putting demands, expectations or a test upon Him.

2. Unconfessed sin

It should be obvious that any unconfessed sin in our lives must be confessed, renounced and repented of before we can expect a loving but exacting Father to bless us with additional benevolences. This does not apply at all to those sins we are not yet aware of within us, but it is clearly applicable to our known iniquities.

3. Doubt or lack of faith

If there is doubt, either in the heart or the head, that the Lord Jesus is sovereign enough to work His will, then we are in effect sitting in judgment as to what He can or can't do and what He will do. In faith we come to the Lord, always believing. The Scripture plainly states, "Ask in faith without any doubting, for the one who doubts...let not that man expect that he will receive anything from the Lord."[2]

4. Demonic interference

It is always in the interest of demonic forces to block any and all spiritual blessings to God's people. These forces do have power, and we should expect to reckon with them. The good news is that we have even greater power given directly to us from our Lord. All demonic spirits are therefore subject to us *in His name,* and we have nothing to fear. This is not a frequent cause of blockage, but we must always be prepared to stand immediately against these forces when interference is indicated. As a matter of standard procedure, satan and his cohorts should always be banished when praying with someone for Jesus' appearance.

5. Questioning

A somewhat rare form of blockage may occur when you begin asking the seeker to describe what he or she is seeing. Instead of relaxing in faith, some people switch into an "intellectual" mode and start questioning you as to what you're asking and why. In addition to questions, they are apt to have a challenging tone. At such times you will need to try to refocus their minds to faith in what the Lord might have for them. Without openness, all efforts may prove to be futile.

6. Rationalization

Your communicant may try to intellectually rationalize everything you ask or say as well as whatever he or she is seeing. This may happen especially if he or she has heard all the psychological jargon during extensive traditional therapy and tries to apply it to his or her spiritual experience.

7. Prior New Age involvement

Visualization and other New Age techniques in which the person may have been involved will likely seem similar to what you are asking him or her to do. Once again you may be questioned. Or the person may simply say, "This is just New Age stuff." These last three forms of blockage may be readily identified because the person will usually question you with a somewhat superior air rather than with a gentle and humble spirit.

8. Outside distraction

Seeing Jesus in the spirit is a very personal experience; therefore it can vary from person to person. Some will see Jesus quickly, easily and surely. For others the pace and certainty are much slower. Therefore it is always good to make sure the room is free of all distractions and bright lights. Timing and other considerations may be important as well. One young mother arranged to call us from Australia at 5 A.M. her time in Melbourne so that her children would still be asleep. This was wise forethought, and it proved to be very effective.

9. Impatience

Not common, but worth mentioning, is the person who wants it to happen *now* and who is unwilling to wait for the Lord's timing.

10. Lack of emotional desire

The Lord is not likely to come where He is not wanted! He knows who truly desires to receive blessings from Him. It seems unlikely for this to happen, but you may find someone who simply doesn't care!

11. Shame and unworthy feelings

Rare are those who feel so dirty, shameful or unworthy that they are not able to see anything. It is as though a big curtain has been dropped in front of them. Such persons are usually ones who have suffered extensive childhood victimization. Their feelings of unworthiness may need to be dealt with first so these people are able to embrace an experience of seeing Jesus in the spirit.

Not so rare, however, are those who see Jesus quite readily but are unwilling to go to Him because they feel so dirty or unworthy. These people are usually much more easily encouraged to go to Him. They can see His arms reaching out and eventually will take the slow, halting steps necessary to get to Him.

131

12. Strong drugs and medication

The power of the Spirit of God is sufficient to cut through any obstruction caused by drugs or medication. There will be times, however, when the person with whom you are praying is under their control and cannot seem to get past the effects. In such cases you may want to postpone the prayer time until later when the effects of the drugs or medication has been reduced. Or you might schedule the prayer time just prior to the normal time for additional medication.

There are other possible blockages, but this list will give you the major ones to watch for. There is one more that I must mention. It is extremely serious, shocking and very real. It will require tender encouragement, ministry, compassion and patience on your part.

13. Valid fear of Jesus

Does that sound like a strange statement? How could anyone have a *valid* fear of Jesus? Unfortunately it is relatively common, especially among certain women, and for them it is very valid. They have a good reason for being unable to trust Jesus; even the sound of His name may be frightening to them. These are the women who have been horrendously violated as little girls in satanic worship rituals.[2] As part of the mind-control techniques that are used in these rituals, a little girl is held or tied to an altar, and a man in a white robe comes into the scene. Perhaps he wears a beard to complete the masquerade. The child is told that this is Jesus and he has come to save her. Instead the impostor removes his robe and proceeds to violate the child while the others stand in a circle taunting and jeering, "See! Even Jesus can't save you! You belong to us!"

That horrible memory has been intentionally planted in the child's mind forever. It is a means satanists use to keep the child loyal to the coven and make her perpetually unable to trust Jesus. As an adult, a person victimized in this manner may understandably have no desire whatsoever to see the living Lord. If the experience is spontaneous, however, the satanic programming crumbles when the person actually meets Jesus in the spirit and looks into His kind and gentle eyes. What a beautiful way to destroy the evil that was intentionally perpetrated upon her as a child!

Gradually or directly, all of the above forms of blockages can be torn down through prayer and by ministering to the emotional and spiritual needs of the individual. But there is one final obstacle that does not necessarily require removal.

14. God knows we are not ready

For reasons only He knows, the time may not be right for Jesus to manifest Himself to a person. Certain issues or considerations may need to be faced or cleaned up first. God is sovereign, and His timing is always right. There will be occasions when improper timing is the only valid reason nothing is seen. If the Spirit shows you that this is the reason, then it must be sufficient until He shows you differently.

Remember, nine out of ten times the person with whom you are praying will come quickly and easily into the presence of Jesus. But there will be other times when he or she simply is not able to perceive anything at all. Don't be frustrated; remember that in some circumstances there will be blockages to seeing Jesus in the spirit. The possibilities above will help you to identify and deal with the causes.

14

Words of Caution and Answers to Some of Your Questions

THIS BEAUTIFUL EXPERIENCE of seeing Jesus in the spirit is neither to be considered a panacea for all emotional problems and struggles, nor is it necessarily for everyone diagnosed with some form of mental illness. On the other hand we don't want to place a limitation on the work of the Holy Spirit and the power of the Lord Jesus Christ to bring healing as He chooses. In everything we do, and in every request we bring before the throne of grace, we must always remember God is sovereign. He determines the results, not us. He decides what is in His will, not us. He chooses the time, the place and the person for the manifestation of His divine physical presence, not us.

Once we accept that it is God who works all things, then we relieve ourselves of any inappropriate sense of responsibility, expectations or guilt of failure when we do not see our hopes fulfilled immediately. When the Lord chooses to withhold His presence for some reason beyond our understanding, it is most important that we not place any burden of failure on ourselves as prayer directors or burden of unworthiness on the one with whom we pray.

Let us fix in our minds on what Jesus said in John 14:21, "He who loves Me...I will love him, and will disclose Myself to him." He says He will disclose Himself. Clearly it His work, not ours. We cannot fail, for nothing that happens is of our doing! We have only the responsibility to pray and ask.

Every day we are learning more of the awesome ability of our Lord to do His work when we ask. I have learned much in the last three months, and I suspect two years from now the understanding and demonstrations of His power will far exceed anything we might even begin to contemplate at this time. As the song says, "Our God is an awesome God." The awesomeness of our Lord far exceeds anything our limited human minds can conceive!

Now let us try to answer some questions you may have and perhaps some you haven't thought about.

1. Is there a risk that the person we pray with may feel worse after the prayer session?

In virtually all situations, that would not be possible. The one exception could be disappointment when the person prayed with had an expectation of seeing Jesus and didn't. This is why we prefer not to anticipate His appearance. We guard against this by never mentioning what we plan to ask Jesus to do for the one with whom we pray. However, if we are asked to pray with a person for the purpose of seeing Jesus, then that person already has an expectation. If, for any of the various reasons given under the preceding chapter on blockages, there is no fulfillment, be prepared to answer the questions and to minister to the disappointment.

In all of our experiences, what takes place is so rewarding, fulfilling and faith-building that the inevitable result never brings people down, but always lifts them up spiritually and emotionally.

2. Is satan apt to try to interfere with such a prayer session and thereby cause grief or disappointment?

The answer is yes. He will do his utmost to disrupt the whole process, including causing outside distractions. He will do all he can to destroy the efforts of healing, encouragement and growth of faith. His aim is always interference and bondage. This is why it is so important to exercise your Christ-given authority over him from the beginning during your initial prayer. Be prepared, however, for he is both wily and persistent and may attempt to re-attack during the prayer time. In such case, in the name of the Lord Jesus Christ, command him to leave. Always do this aloud, never silently.

At the same time, however, we are constantly in prayer asking the Holy Spirit to guide and direct us. There are times when we feel stumped. Nothing happens although it seems something should be taking place. Ask the One who always hears. Often just the right word or step comes to mind simply because we asked.

3. Is there a risk that what the person sees is from satan and not from Jesus at all?

As long as we have bound satan, commanded him to leave and asked Jesus to manifest His presence, what follows will be from the Lord. The prince of darkness is the deceiver, and we already removed him! Therefore it is safe to trust in the revelations from the Lord. No spiritual force can substitute a lie or error for the truth. He cannot elbow the Lord aside.

There is one other form of interference that bears mentioning — one which few of our readers will likely confront. When we pray with a person who has suffered horrendous satanic ritual abuse and still has "parts" or "alters" who are "loyal to the coven," the parts and alters will do all they can to cause interference from the inside, preventing the person from seeing, hearing or receiving the blessings the Lord has for them.[1] When one has experience dealing with these parts, they are surprisingly simple to deal with. If you find yourself in need of help or consultation with this kind of situation, you are welcome to call our ministry phone line to receive the name of someone you can call for help.

4. I have heard there are no such things as alter personalities or parts. If there are no such things, why would I need to be concerned with this? What is the truth?

Yes, there are sincere people who do not believe in the existence of alter personalities. I once received a letter from a Christian psychiatrist telling me there were no such things. There are three possible reasons for this position: 1) those who hold to this use a different term for the same thing, 2) they simply have had no experience helping such a person or 3) they didn't recognize the existence of alters when they did in fact encounter them.

Knowledgeable practitioners of mental and emotional health, Christian or secular, are fully aware of the existence of such parts. Many valid and scholarly books and articles have been written on the subject. To deny their reality does not change the fact. It only affects what we choose to accept.

5. How can I, without professional training and experience, recognize the possibility of the presence of a part?

There are three fairly simple ways of determining this.

*   You can simply ask, "Have you ever felt that there is a hurting (or angry) little girl (or boy) inside you?" A strong, definitive answer such as, "Oh, I know there is!" invariably will indicate the existence of another personality. You can then ask the Lord Jesus to reunite all the parts of the person with whom you are praying.

*   During the prayer time when the person is in the place that the Lord has chosen for the meeting, if that person

reverts to acting or speaking as a child it may indicate the existence of another personality. You can ask, "How old are you?" to determine if it is indeed a child. You can further confirm the scene by asking, "What are you wearing?" Use the illustrations included in this book as guidelines for how to proceed while praying with someone.

- If the voice responding to you in the meeting place is very different and noticeably a younger-sounding voice, you are probably talking to a part.

6. Do I need to know if there is a part inside? How essential is this?

It is not essential, but it is often helpful. Remember all these encounters are within the exclusive domain of the sovereign Lord. He makes all the decisions. He does all the work. He will guide us in questioning the individual. He will guide us to the healing. There is no loss if a step or area of healing is not addressed the first time. There is usually a second opportunity to bring the person into the Lord's presence.

By determining during prayer time that a part exists inside the individual with whom you are praying (even if the person has never wondered about it), we are able to specifically ask the Lord to bring about a reunion in much the same way as we have described in the true illustrations in this book.

7. What if I encounter a part who does not want to be reunited? Or what if the person I'm praying with knows there is a part but wants nothing to do with that part? Should I push them or force them to reunite?

If you pray with many people you are apt to run into both situations. There are many reasons why a part would not want to reunite with the other part or parts.

Try to put yourself in the emotional realm of the little part.

Through compassionate and loving questions and wise words of encouragement the Spirit will bring that part to the point of a desire to be one with the adult part. After all, God created us to be one. The presence of parts is usually the result of a childhood trauma and the part becomes a coping mechanism to deal with the trauma.

When the part calls the adult self to come and be with Jesus too, the adult can hold the child part until the child is comfortable. At the appropriate time you can ask the little one, "Would you like to ask Jesus to make the two of you one?" For a little child who has never felt loved, this act of holding and loving may break down all the barriers so a reunion can take place.

If the adult person doesn't want to have anything to do with the little part, a common reason expressed is that the part is "too dirty." For example, a younger girl's dress is dirty and her hair is a mess. These criticisms are expressed by the adult without ever stopping to think that the younger part is a part of herself — the one who has always had to cope with the bad stuff. This can be true even when the adult doesn't remember anything about the bad stuff! What then is the easy and simple solution? Suggest that the child part ask Jesus to make her clean. "Lord Jesus, will You make me clean?" In an instant the child will be clean, combed and arrayed in a sparkling, clean dress!

Thus, the reason for rejection by the adult has been removed by the Lord Himself, and you can proceed.

If there is a resistance to reunion, encourage but do not try to force the reunion. Frankly, you can't. You do not do the reuniting — the Lord Jesus does. He is both sovereign and omniscient, and He will not do it if there is not agreement between the two parts. He always knows when the time is right.

8. Should I pray with people who have deep emotional problems, for example, people who experience hallucinations?

Once again the answer is in the Lord's response to your prayers. If there is no question of the Lord's direction, feel free to proceed. Take all the precautions already given and then allow the Lord to guide your every step. Don't proceed in the flesh. If things do not seem to be proceeding smoothly you can tell that you're operating in the flesh. If you say or think, "I'm going to do this," or "I'm going to be successful at this!" you are in the flesh. Whenever the focus is on what *you* are going to do you can be sure you are depending on your ability or gift and not on the Lord. You are operating apart from Him, and you can do nothing!

Finally, I have never found a situation when prayer hurts. I don't believe there is any such thing as too much prayer!

9. After the prayer experience, what is next? What is my continuing responsibility?

Please remember that coming into the presence of the living Lord is a bona fide, real experience, but it is not the end to all ministry, counseling and recovery. It is, however, a firm platform from which continuing healing and ministry may proceed. It encourages the person that God is real, that there is hope, and that they are valuable and loved. Who better to experience genuine embraceable love from than from the Lord Jesus Christ?

If the person with whom you pray has been counseling with you regularly, by all means as the Lord leads, continue if he or she desires, and as you see the need. Not every person will need or even desire ongoing help. Ultimately it is the responsibility of each individual to walk their own healing journey.

In Matthew 11:28 Jesus urges each hurting and heavy-laden person to come to Him. They must come to Him on their own, but we can be encouragers and exhorters. Second Corinthians 7:1 further tells us, "Let us cleanse ourselves from all defilement of flesh and spirit." Your friend must rely on the Lord and not on you! But the Lord does call us to be instruments through which He can minister and bring His comfort to His sheep that have been wounded.

For some people the changes that take place will be so dramatic that the shackles are loosed, the bonds are broken and they can proceed effectively on their own. This is especially true of more mature Christians.

10. Does everybody need someone to pray with them? Can they not pray on their own?

Yes, of course people can pray on their own. And yes, the Lord Jesus does bring healing to many when they pray on their own. However, those who know nothing about seeing Jesus in the spirit don't know what to ask. Oftentimes we have not because we ask not. Remember the paralytic at the pool of Bethesda? He was unable to get into the water before the others. He needed someone to help him, and he had no one until Jesus came along and healed him right then and there. Sometimes we too need someone to help us.

11. If I feel led to pray someone into His presence, how much time should I allow?

Plan to set aside at least an hour. You may not need it all, but you surely don't want to have to interrupt your session with, "Well, we'll have to break it off now. I have to go and pick up the kids." You will need time at the beginning to talk about the individual's concerns and to learn how to help him or her in prayer. This might take twenty or thirty minutes. Then the actual prayer time might be as little as ten minutes but could easily be half an hour. This is followed by a time of ministering about what the person has just seen and experienced.

Confirm everything the individual saw and reported to you. Alert the person to the fact that within twenty-four hours satan may try to steal the blessing by saying, "This never really happened;" "You imagined it" or "The person praying for you put it all in your mind." In addition your friend may have questions to present to you. Suggest that as soon as possible that person write down the complete details of everything he or she saw and heard. On that same day, before the memory begins to blur, specifically make sure the person writes down the exact words the Lord spoke. This afterglow time of ministry can easily take between twenty or thirty minutes.

An hour will disappear very rapidly! Aside from the sinner who repents, I can think of no other ministry experience that is quite as rewarding as praying a lamb into the presence of the Shepherd and therefore being a participant in their experience of healing.

12. What if we are in the presence of the Lord and for some unexpected reason there is an interruption? Can we just leave the scene or will some damage be done?

No. I can't conceive any circumstance where any damage could be done by being in the presence of the living Lord, even if that scene is interrupted or broken off. It is actually possible on some occasions to go back at a later time to that very scene. The one thing that we must continually remember is that this entire process of spiritual manifestation is totally in the province of the Lord. He is completely capable of continuing or completing the work He began. Certainly we do not want to rush someone out of the scene with Him because we have some other agenda or because time is up. That is another reason to make sure you have sufficient time to finish what you have started.

Finally, remember the admonition: It is the Lord who does the work (see Phil. 1:6). We do nothing but pray and ask. We totally depend on Him. He will give us the questions to ask and the insight we need. The Spirit will prompt us with answers and direction when we need them. The Lord waits upon us to ask. "Ye have not, because ye ask not" (James 4:2, KJV).

13. As I have read some of the stories of hurts and testimonies of healings, I have experienced some deep emotions stirring in me! I don't know where they come from or what they mean. Does that mean I might have suffered something similar as a child, and, if so, what should I do?

We often say, "Our emotions remember what our minds have forgotten." Yes, those deep emotions could be very significant and should not be ignored. To help you identify and understand what you may be feeling, we would strongly recommend that you prayerfully read our two books written for someone just like yourself: *Freeing Your Mind From Memories That Bind* and *The Promise of Healing*. Both books are published by Thomas Nelson and are available through any Christian bookstore.

15

Other Wondrous Works of the Lord

A VERY DETERMINED young mother sent a letter to our office by Federal Express to attract attention, I am sure. Debbie,* a former state beauty pageant contestant, sent a picture of herself, her son and her husband. Looking at Debbie's picture, one wonders how anyone could have edged her out for the title that year. Debbie's impressive résumé also listed two years as a TV reporter and broadcast news anchor. Her husband had a lengthy list of successful career credentials as well, including several years as a professional athlete! This looked like the successful, young, all-American couple, not a family with problems.

The letter Debbie sent was addressed to Florence. However, like many other such letters, it promptly found its way to my desk.

* Not her real name

Dear Mrs. Littauer,

I'm sure you receive hundreds of letters each year asking advice and direction, but I pray that you will read mine and somehow find time to help me. I am the mother of a precious two-year-old son. It was soon after his birth that I started having a good deal of trouble with depression, stomach problems, nightmares and a host of other problems. (These were all present before but intensified with his birth.) Also, since a few months after my husband and I were married (seven years ago) I've had pain and intimacy problems.

I am a Christian and God has miraculously led me to discover so much. He led me to read *Freeing Your Mind From Memories That Bind.* I was unable to locate a Christian counselor in my area who specialized in past abuse. I have since read all of your and Mr. Littauer's books, most recently *The Promise of Healing.* Now I am in turmoil. I prayed for memory retrieval, and God helped me remember two incidences of sexual molestation of which I had no previous recollection. (I suspected that something had happened even before the memories because of the dreams and the bad feelings I get, but I couldn't accept this before).

I'm searching for competent Christian counsel, and I pray that you will see me. My husband has a business trip to San Diego with his company in less than three weeks, and I will come with him if there is any way you can see us. We'll do anything! I checked these dates with someone at CLASS, and she suggested I write you about the possibility of our getting together.

Believe me, I have sought numerous Christian counselors in our area and have come up with those who practice transcendental meditation and yoga, those who seduce clients and one who is a member of a lesbian alliance. I am at my wit's end, and I just

145

know you can help! My marriage seems to be deteriorating because of my intense anger; my husband doesn't know how to respond to or deal with it.

The good news is God is already using me by sending so many people to me who have been sexually abused or who have children who have been abused. Before any of this surfaced I had a great desire to help people and started working on a master's degree in counseling. Now I see how He plans to use that desire, and there is such a need!

Now if I can just help myself and my marriage! I pray that you can find time to work with us. If there is any possibility of our meeting, please contact me by phone or voice mail.

I pray that I will hear from you soon so I can book a flight for me and my son.

Sincerely,
Debbie[1]

How does one respond to such a letter? Do I throw it in the pile to be answered sometime when there is time? From the date of her husband's conference in San Diego, it was obvious that Debbie had just a few days to book a discount air ticket. I had already ascertained that I would be in the office the days they would be in San Diego. I had to call. I left a message on her answering machine.

Less than a month later, an attractive young couple, exuding every apparent confidence, walked into our office with their adorable two-year-old son. No one would ever have guessed upon looking at them that they had a care in the world. But they had *more* than a care. Here was a young, vivacious mother who was hiding and suppressing a raging anger within.

After exchanging the usual pleasantries to make them feel at ease, we plunged quickly into the real reason for their appointment. They needed help and had traveled a long way to find it.

Debbie, through her own answered prayers, had already learned the root cause of her anger, but now she was seeking the healing and cleansing the Lord Jesus promises in Scripture. After spending some time discussing the issues, we focused on the plain fact that only the Lord Jesus Christ can effect real healing. Soon we were ready to pray. What the Lord did that afternoon for Debbie was something she will never forget and will never cease to be grateful for.

After we had both prayed, almost instantly Debbie saw herself standing on a beautiful ocean beach on a bright sunny day. She described herself as about five years old, wearing a little sundress and no shoes. Her feet wiggled in the cool, comfortable sand. She was alone on the beach, until she saw a gentle, safe figure in a pure white robe. She recognized Jesus and went to Him. He held her two little hands in His big, soft, safe hands. Debbie saw "the scars that cut so deep." She knew she could trust Jesus because He understood pain — He had been hurt too. He picked the little girl up, held her closely and said, "I love you. I will be at your side forever."

Realizing that the hurting little girl was the inside part of her who had endured all the childhood trauma, I asked, "Where is big Debbie?"

"I don't know. She's not here."

"Don't you think she would like to be with Jesus, too?" I asked.

"Well, yes, I think so."

"Why don't you ask Jesus to call her over? He can do that."

"OK. Jesus, would You ask big Debbie to come over and be with us?"

Only a few seconds passed before I heard little Debbie say, "She's coming over now," and then, "She's right here next to us now."

After a few moments had passed and they were feeling comfortable with each other, I asked, "Would you like big Debbie to hold you? I think she'd like to."

"Yes, I'd like her to. Big Debbie, would you like to hold me, too?"

With a smile, big Debbie reached out and took her little self, little Debbie, from Jesus and cuddled her in her arms. Little Debbie was still the reporter, the one who was speaking to me.

"She loves you too, doesn't she?" I asked the little one.

Little Debbie was now secure and comfortable in big Debbie's arms. For the first time she felt safe with big Debbie. She had always felt before that big Debbie hated her because she was dirty, but now that was all being changed.

Sensing now that they might both be ready to move ahead, I asked little Debbie, "Debbie, would you like to ask Jesus to make you and big Debbie one?"

Without a moment's hesitation, little Debbie asked, "Jesus, would You make the two of us one?"

After a few seconds' pause, I asked, "Has something happened?"

A different voice answered this time. "Little Debbie's not here anymore."

"Where did she go?"

"She's gone! Jesus reached His arms out and put them around the two of us, and she just went inside me!"

We had just seen one more of the wondrous works of our God. In that short time, He reunified the personalities that had been fragmented at the time of the traumas. But although we had experienced a miracle of healing, I felt there was more that Jesus would do for Debbie.

"Debbie, is there anything else you would like to ask Jesus to do for you?" One of the great concerns Debbie expressed in her letter was her intense anger. Such anger was understandable, considering her childhood victimizations. Nevertheless, it needed to be cleansed to have genuine harmony, and Jesus said He would do it. "Would you like to ask Jesus to take away your anger?"

Debbie was still on the beach, seeing Jesus in the spirit. She was still standing there in His presence. "Jesus, could You please take away my anger?"

I watched the adult woman sitting in my office with her eyes closed. From the quizzical expression on her face, it was apparent something was surely taking place out there on that beach. "Debbie, tell me, is something happening?"

Almost in disbelief she responded, "Jesus is reaching inside my chest and taking this ugly black stuff out of my heart!"

I was not surprised. This was what I expected might happen. "What is He doing with it?"

"He turned around and threw it far out into the ocean. It just disappeared. It's gone forever!" Debbie replied in amazement. Debbie thanked Jesus for appearing to her, for reuniting her with little Debbie and for taking away her anger. They visited together for several more minutes and then it was time for Jesus to leave her. As He left He said, "but I will always be with you."

Debbie opened her eyes. She was awestruck. She had actually seen the Lord Jesus! In that short span of time, He had completed two miraculous works for her. First, He had cleansed and reunified the hurting little girl with the adult personality, and second, He had removed her debilitating anger with one sweep of His arm. It was gone! She knew it was real. Her face was glowing. God had fulfilled her prayerful desires. She would be going home a completely changed young woman.

Two weeks later she wrote another letter. This one echoed the changes I had seen take place during our meeting in San Diego:

> Dear Fred,
>
> I don't know how many times I've tried to start this letter but couldn't! How can we thank you for showing us the healing power of Jesus? I've wanted to tell everyone I meet, but there is just no way to describe the miracle that took place in your office that day!
>
> Every morning I wake up and realize that the anger isn't here and it isn't coming back! A whole new dimension has been added to our spiritual lives now that we have met Jesus personally and come to understand the power we have over satan in Jesus' name.

I'm so glad you warned us, though, that satan would probably attack us because he really has. But we've been ready for him. Of course satan always tries to attack by causing me to worry about whether or not anyone has abused our son, but we just keep on rebuking the devil and praying for his healing. Thank you again for showing us how to do that!

I've included a poem I wrote on the trip home that captures a little of the incredible feelings I experienced that day.

Thank you for a wonderful evening.

In Christ's love,
Debbie

(For Debbie's poem, "Now I've Seen Eternity," see page 153.)

I witnessed another wondrous healing of anger one afternoon when some dear friends were visiting with their eight-year-old son. I was particularly close to this young boy, who called me Poppa Fred. Little Bradley* had two areas of struggle. One was an intense anger problem that might erupt at any time with little, if any, notice. The other problem was intense and horrendous dreams of huge spiders. His parents attributed the dreams to the kinds of things he tended to watch on television. I strongly suspected there was another cause; such dreams always have a root source.

On this particular afternoon, I felt led by the Spirit to ask Bradley to come into my study to pray with me. This day we were to deal with the anger. Even though he was deeply engrossed in his favorite pastime, watching television, he came readily at my suggestion.

After we both prayed I asked him to keep his eyes closed. Then I asked, "Bradley, do you see anything?"

"Yes, Poppa Fred, I'm on a cloud in the sky!" I knew Jesus always chooses the sites for His appearance, so I was surely not

---

* Not his real name

going to suggest that He could have selected a more realistic locale!

It was not long before Bradley reported that he saw another cloud coming toward him and that a man was standing in the center of it. He had on a bright white robe. "It's the Lord Jesus, Poppa Fred!"

Bradley even saw the scars on His wrists.

As the two clouds docked together, Bradley went toward the outstretched arms of the Savior. Jesus picked him up, held him close and told Bradley He loved him and would always love him. I encouraged little Bradley to ask the Lord Jesus to remove his anger.

"Lord Jesus, can You take away my anger?" Virtually the same thing happened that Debbie had experienced. The living Lord reached into Bradley's chest and took out what he described as "long, dark-red, ugly stuff."

"What is Jesus doing with it, Bradley?"

"He's rolling it up into a ball, and now...He just threw it away off the cloud. It's gone!" Eight-year-old Bradley had received the very same healing. He ran excitedly to tell his parents what had happened, "I've just seen Jesus, and He took a lot of anger out of me!" he exclaimed.

His parents were not quite prepared for this revelation from their eight-year-old and hardly knew how to respond. "That's wonderful, honey," was all they could muster up.

I learned that Jesus used this method to remove anger during a time of prayer with a young man in his thirties. After he met Jesus inside a house, Jesus took him by his left arm and they walked out into a pleasant suburban neighborhood. As they were walking side by side on the sidewalk, Jesus suddenly stopped and turned to face the young man. Without saying a word, He reached into his chest and pulled out "ugly black stuff." Then the young man said, "He's throwing it away, farther than even Roger Clemens, [the famed Boston Red Sox pitcher] could ever have thrown it!" Not only did the Lord clean out the young man's anger, but He used that time to teach me, demonstrating another of the many ways in which He works.

Since that initial incident there have been many similar experiences. We have learned the truth of James 4:2, "Ye have not, because ye ask not" (KJV). We have learned to ask!

There are many other things the Lord will gladly do for His children when we ask. One of them is to remove inordinate fear. Perhaps what He is really doing is removing the person's vulnerability to oppressive fear, because fear can be easily and quickly dealt with by casting out the "spirit of fear." Such fear is always from the enemy and is therefore readily dispatched.[2] Whenever there is an "open window" or vulnerability of any kind, satan always will attempt to exploit this weakness.

Jesus will also perform physical healings if we ask, although in our experience it has been mostly the healing of emotional issues. He will heal compulsions, and He will heal depression.

When there is an apparent inability to forgive someone who has caused deep pain, the Lord Jesus can take away the obstruction and enable the person to forgive the one who has caused the hurt. Forgiveness is a scriptural necessity. Even the Lord's prayer reminds us to forgive those who have sinned against us.[3] There is a wise saying that points out, the acid of anger eats away only at the container.

Another area in which we have frequently seen remarkable healing is in what is now often called post-traumatic abortion syndrome. It is the residual emotional turbulence that usually appears many years after someone has been through an experience that was erroneously described as "a routine surgical procedure." Jesus wants to heal this pain that seems to refuse to go away. How He does this will be described in another chapter.

In short, Jesus can and probably will heal almost anything we ask of Him. The ways and the works of our Lord are so wondrous, who can conceive them? He continues to thrill us with new demonstrations of His awesome healing power. We have learned to ask and not be shy about what we wish for.

Now I've Seen Eternity

You were there for me, O Gentle Healer,
when my soul was wrought with pain.
You were there for me and touched my hand,
though with nothing for You to gain.
O Majesty, O Wondrous One,
You showed Yourself to me,
A gift no one could ever describe,
was given there to me.
A little girl with pain so deep,
pain she couldn't see,
a hurt and anger buried within
that no one else could reach,
Until that glorious, wonderful day
You met me there on the beach,
and I stood in awe in the cool white sand,
and surveyed Your hair, Your robe, Your hands.
I saw the scars that cut so deep
and prove Your love to me,
I saw the pure white robe and hair,
only from heaven could they be.
You stood and held both hands of mine
and looked into my eyes.
You told me that You loved me
and would be forever by my side.
I asked that You would heal me...
that little hurting child...
You pulled out pain and anger,
the dark black deep inside.
You changed my life forever,
and gave me a precious treasure,
For now I've seen eternity,
Just in smaller measure!

Debbie

16

Jesus Heals a Mother and Then Her Son

This story by Gwen,* a young mother who asked to meet with me at a women's retreat, is beautiful enough. What makes it even more profoundly touching is that after Jesus met and reunited the two Gwens, Gwen was able to minister Jesus' healing love to her four-year-old son, Daryl.** Afterward the psychiatrists at his counseling center were so confounded by Daryl's rapid improvement! Gwen tells her story and then her son's in her own words.

For many years I was plagued with feelings that my childhood still had a hold on me. I found it hard to accept God's love and His forgiveness. I had serious doubts and found it hard to believe that He would come to my rescue if I needed Him.

* Not her real name
** Not his real name

Hoping to find help, I asked Fred at the conference if I could meet with him.

I shared enough of the details of my turbulent childhood for him to get the picture. I told him that as a child I would sit alone in the dark at night and talk to God. It was the only time I felt safe.

As we continued talking, Fred asked me a question no one had ever asked me before. The wisdom God must have given him would make a profound impact on me before we finished our meeting.

"Gwen, have you ever felt as though there was a hurting little girl inside of you?"

"Yes!" I answered, somewhat amazed.

Fred asked, "Does she have a name?"

I began to cry. It was as if a little girl inside me stood up, and I suddenly took notice of her. She had always been there, but I had forgotten about her. Frankly, I didn't even want to think about her.

Fred asked again, very tenderly, "What is your name?"

The little voice inside me answered, "Scared."

"Is that your real name? I'll bet you have another very pretty name."

The little voice again answered, "Little Gwen."

"How old are you, Little Gwen?" I remember Fred had such compassion in his voice. He seemed to understand all of Little Gwen's pain and fears.

"I'm seven."

"Where are you now, Little Gwen?"

"I'm in my bedroom. I'm hiding."

"Tell me, why are you hiding? Are you afraid?"

"Yes, I'm scared. I'm scared of my daddy."

"Why are you scared of your daddy?"

"Because he's so big and so mean and he yells at me all the time. He always tells me everything is my fault!"

"Is it really your fault?"

"Yes, it is my fault, because I do everything wrong."

"Little Gwen, I don't really think that's true. I don't think everything is your fault. Do you know who Jesus is?"

"I think so."

"Well, Little Gwen, Jesus wants to help you. Would you like Him to help you?"

"Yes, that would be OK."

Fred asked me to keep my eyes closed, and then Fred prayed. I heard him mention some scriptures in his prayer, but he didn't recite the verses. He didn't really even mention God or Jesus by name. As he prayed, I felt a light and a warmth come around my head. It was almost as if two hands gently reached out and pulled back big Gwen in a very loving way, and now I was very much in the background, watching. At the end of his prayer, Fred asked God to take me to a safe place. He waited, and then he asked, "Where are you, Little Gwen?"

"I'm still in my room." But even as I spoke I started to cry out in surprise and delight. It was actually Little Gwen speaking, but I was conscious of it all and heard everything. My childhood room was done in harsh shades of blue, and it was very ugly. But before my eyes I was transported, it seemed, to a very different room, big and beautiful like a room in an English manor house. Everything was white. There was a beautiful little girl's canopy bed in the middle of the room, with a thin, white, ruffled-eyelet cover on it. In my real childhood bed, I would pile on as many blankets as I could find and sleep or hide under them in an attempt to feel safe. This bed had only the one blanket on it, and I realized there was nothing to hide from in this room! It was a big room with one large window.

Fred asked, "Do you see anyone in the room?"

I said, "No, but there is a window."

"Can you see if there is anything outside the window?"

"I don't know, but I can go and check." I ran to the window and looked out. There was a beautiful white bird circling in the air near the window and a pond surrounded by a large green lawn. There was a person down there by the pond, quite far away.

"There's a person down there," I told Fred. "He's wearing a white dress!"

"Do you know who that man is?"

"I think it's Jesus. Yes, it is Him! He wants me to come outside."

Suddenly all the feelings of fear and failure were starting to overwhelm me. I felt abandoned by God. He wanted me to do something, and I didn't know how to do it. I started to cry. "He wants me to come out, but I don't know how!"

My tears stopped, and I started to laugh with joy. Fred asked, "What is happening, Little Gwen?"

"The big white bird came into my room, and I'm riding down to Jesus on its back! Oh! He is so happy! Jesus is so happy; I've never seen anyone so happy!"

"What is happening now, Little Gwen?"

"Jesus is holding His arms out to me. He's hugging me. He is holding my head against His chest. I am overwhelmed with love and joy. He's saying to me that He loves me, that He always loved me. He says that I am not a bad girl and that even when I was alone at night, He was there with me."

Then Fred asked, "Where is big Gwen now?"

"She's outside too, over there."

"Can she come over to you and Jesus?"

"Yes, she's coming...She's standing now on one side of Jesus, and I'm on the other...He has one arm around each of us."

I started to cry, and Fred asked, "What's the matter, Little Gwen? Why are you crying?"

"I can see that she doesn't like me!"

"Who doesn't like you?"

"Big Gwen doesn't like Little Gwen."

"Do you think big Gwen would like to hold you?"

I waited to see if she would. "No, she doesn't want to!"

"What's happening now?" Fred asked again.

"Jesus is telling her it's OK to love me. He said I'm not bad."

I started to cry again but this time they were happy tears. "Did something just happen?" Fred asked.

"We are all hugging. Jesus' smile is so big. He's saying that it's OK for us to have fun. It's OK to play now."

After a while Fred asked, "Who's there now?"

"It's me, big Gwen. When Jesus hugged us and we hugged each other, Little Gwen just went inside! We're one now! Jesus is telling me to read Psalm 139. He says it's His promise for me, and when I read it I will know He never left me, and He never will. He is telling me to always believe that He loves me no matter what. Now He is leaving. He is going to the sky. His face is so white. There is white all around Him. He has a red-and-green scarf around His neck."

Now I no longer distance myself from Little Gwen and my wounded childhood. I have chosen to love and accept her and every part of myself. My feelings of abandonment and rejection have all been washed away by the love of Jesus. When I looked into His eyes, I knew a love and felt a peace that no one can ever take from me. I have dedicated my life to helping other broken children, both big and small, find their way to the One who can make them free.

Jesus on the Couch

After my own experience of seeing Jesus in the spirit, I wondered if I could pray with my four-year-old son, Daryl, in the same way Fred had prayed with me to ask Jesus to come and bring healing to him also. Though he was only four years old, Daryl had already been showing signs of some very erratic behavior for many months. My husband and I were aware that his grandfather had molested him about a year before. We finally decided to seek help and took him to a psychiatric clinic for evaluation and counseling. After they met with us, they set him up on a weekly schedule of counseling. Fortunately this was covered by our medical insurance.

One afternoon I sat down with Daryl and prayed. I asked God to bring to his remembrance the scene of his violation by his Pawpa. I prayed for God to take Daryl back in his mind to the time when Pawpa had hurt him.

When I asked him where he was, Daryl said, "I'm on the couch."

"How old are you? Can you tell me?"

"Yes, I'm 'liddiler.' I'm just two or three."

"Is anyone there with you?" I asked him.

"I see Mawmaw; she's making soup."

"Daryl, do you see anything else?"

"I see the TV."

"What is on the TV? Can you tell me?"

"The dalmatian movie."

"Is there anyone on the couch with you?"

"Yes, Pawpa."

"What is Pawpa doing?"

"He's trying to pull down my pants."

"How do you feel about that?"

"Bad and scared."

"What is he doing now?"

"He's laughing and showing my bum to Mawmaw. She's telling him to put me down."

I was thankful that God had already shown Daryl that much, but I felt we had seen enough. I then prayed and asked God to take Pawpa off the couch. I wanted it to be a safe place for Daryl. I then suggested to him that we go back to the couch, and he agreed.

"Is anyone on the couch with you now?"

Daryl said no. I smiled and thanked God! Then I prayed silently and asked Jesus to come to Daryl and touch him with His love.

I then said, "Daryl, I think something wonderful is going to happen."

Suddenly Daryl exclaimed to me, "Mommy, Jesus is on the couch with me!"

Trying to act surprised, I said, "That's wonderful! What is Jesus doing?"

"He wants to give me a hug."

"That's great. You can go to Jesus."

"What's happening now?"

"Jesus is telling me that He loves me so much...Now He's putting His hands on my head! Oooh, I like to be with Jesus."

"Daryl, dear, is anything else happening?"

"Yes, Mommy, He picked me up and now I'm riding on His back and He's taking me back to our house."

Jesus had come just as He said He would, even to my little son. Right away we noticed changes in Daryl. I knew then not only had Jesus appeared to Daryl, but healing had taken place when He put His hands on Daryl's head.

At our next appointment at the clinic, the psychiatrists studied Daryl carefully. They were amazed at the changes in him. They began congratulating themselves for the great work they had done for him. The only problem was they couldn't figure out just what they had done that had been so effective! I knew, and I thanked the Lord Jesus for healing my son![1]

The Lord had used this young mother to bring her own little son into His presence. She exclaimed to me, "Fred, isn't God too wonderful?"

God has now given Gwen an effective ministry of working in her home area to pray with children who have suffered childhood traumas similar to what her own son endured.

The Psalmist's Description of the Lord

O Lord, you have searched me and you know me.
You know when I sit down and when I rise;
you perceive my thoughts from afar.
You discern my going out and my lying down;
you are familiar with all my ways.
Before a word is on my tongue
You know it completely, O Lord.

You hem me in, behind and before;
you have laid your hand upon me.
Such knowledge is too wonderful for me,
too lofty for me to attain.

Where can I go from your Spirit?
Where can I flee from your presence?
If I go up to the heavens, you are there;
if I make my bed in the depths, you are there.
If I rise on the wings of the dawn,
if I settle on the far side of the sea,
even there your hand will guide me,
your right hand will hold me fast.

If I say, "Surely the darkness will hide me
and the light become night around me,"
even the darkness will not be dark to you;
the night will shine like the day,
for darkness is as light to you.

For you created my innermost being;
you knit me together in my mother's womb.
I praise you because I am fearfully and wonderfully
        made;
your works are wonderful,
I know that full well.

My frame was not hidden from you
when I was made in the secret place.
When I was woven together in the depths of the
     earth,
Your eyes saw my unformed body.
All the days ordained for me were written in your
     book
before one of them came to be.

—Psalm 139:1-14, NIV, emphasis added

17

"There's Nothing More We Can Do for You"

After her third stay in the psychiatric hospital, Kathy* was told, "There's nothing more we can do for you. You are just going to have to learn to live with your condition." Medical science had done all it could for Kathy. Now there was no more hope, no more help; no healing could be offered.

Just two years later Kathy is as vibrant and healthy a Christian woman as you might ever hope to find. You can meet her now as she tells her story in her own words.

Suicide watch. How did I ever wind up on suicide watch? Drowning in desperate pain and suffering, there seemed to be only one escape; I wanted to take it. What had happened? Why was my life so out of control? How did I ever get here?

* Not her real name

There's nothing more we can do for you.

Over and over those words kept going through my mind. After years of undergoing psychotherapy, group therapy, every medication on the market and the dreaded shock treatments, this was the outcome. I already felt helpless; now I was told there was no hope.

Initially hospitalized for flu and dehydration, I was later diagnosed with anorexia and depression. For the next several years, hospitalizations for depressive episodes and treatments by various physicians became almost routine. The results were always the same. I would feel healthy and happy for a time, sometimes weeks, sometimes months. Then, without warning, my symptoms would begin again. Each time the days dawned drearier, and the depression was deeper. Gathering all the courage I could muster, I finally asked one of the doctors the question that had plagued me, "What else can be done? Will this ever end?" That's when I received the answer I had feared.

The doctor stated plainly, "There's nothing more we can do for you. We've done all we can."

He went on to explain that depression was cyclical. I would have some good days, he said, but the bad days would be back. I would probably be in treatment for the rest of my life. Feeling dead on the inside, I voiced my thoughts that if this was what living would be like, I no longer wanted my life. It wasn't fair to put my family through this. The cost to them and to our finances was too much. A funeral would be cheaper than all the medical costs. After saying this, the next thing I knew, I was in the intensive care unit of the psychiatric hospital being watched for signs of impending suicide.

I had always felt surrounded by struggle. Despite a wonderful husband and sweet, young children, I was weary and worn out inside. I desperately wanted love and approval. I tried to do all the right things, playing all those roles that were expected of me, from social secretary to compassionate caregiver. If I performed properly maybe everyone would praise me. If I could just be all everyone wanted me to be maybe I would get the love I desired. If I looked like a success maybe I would be satisfied. Instead I was miserable; I felt like a fake, thinking if my family and friends knew what I was *really* like they wouldn't like me.

One evening I was chatting with my cousin Jeremy,* a born-again Christian. I knew he would listen to me as I lamented about my life. He had been through some tough times himself. I asked him how his life had become meaningful and worth living. He told me about our living Lord. Jeremy said that when he asked Jesus to be his Savior he finally felt peace. He had been so fearful and filled with sin and selfishness until Jesus gave him faith and a sense of purpose for his life. That's what I wanted: faith that things would be better and a purpose for my life. I knew I needed a Savior; I needed Jesus.

In the wee hours of the morning, Jeremy and I joined hands across his kitchen table, and I asked Jesus to forgive me for all that I had done wrong. I asked Him to be the Lord of my life and to guide me through it. When I finished praying, I smiled. I knew my life would be different. I *knew* the love that the Lord had for me.

I expected life to be good and perfect. It *was* good, but it certainly wasn't perfect! I made mistakes as I still went on my own merry way. I did what I thought were the right things. I tried to be flawless not only for me but for the Lord. I felt that I kept falling short, especially in one particular area. I decided to attend a Bible study in my neighborhood; I was eager to meet and share with other Christians. After attending for several weeks, I felt fairly safe and secure — that is, until I confessed to them that I had an area of real weakness: I smoked cigarettes. To admit my bad habit to them was a mistake! They pointed at me, told me that a true Christian doesn't smoke and gave me a mini-sermon on how evil I was for doing such a thing. I never went back. I knew I'd made a terrible mistake; I'd let them see the real me. I felt ridiculed and rejected. They no longer liked or accepted me. I didn't measure up. My value seemed to be in what I did, not in who I was. Did the Lord feel the same way?

I resolved to try to do better; I would be perfect. What I

* Not his real name

lacked in my social performance, I would make up for in my family functions. I wanted people to notice how wonderful my home and family were; then, I thought, people would approve of and appreciate me—and they did. I vowed to maintain the perfect home, keep it meticulously clean (even with three little children), be the perfect hostess, teach my children to always display perfect manners, perform charity work and always be eager, energetic, enthusiastic and smile sweetly, no matter what the situation. Above all, I resolved to never again let my true feelings show through because they were far less than perfect! If I put on the mask of perfection and strict discipline, I believed life would be marvelous.

The harder I tried, the more hurtful my life became. The tougher it got, the tougher I got. I kept telling myself I could handle it. I could do it all and do it right. I was miserable, and I made my family suffer for it. No matter what they did, it didn't measure up to my standards. Rather than expressing love and concern for my children, I treated them with criticism and condemnation. Their eyes reflected the pain my depression was causing them. They were entering into adolescence and drifting away from me. I was feeling more pain in myself and inflicting more pain on my family. I felt alone and angry. My husband traveled and was hardly ever home. I remember telling him that I didn't get married to be single! Life was the pits; I was discouraged, discontented and depressed. The personality mask I wore to survive was now suffocating me. Before long I had sunk to the darkest depths of despair, and the hospital suicide watch began.

That night in my hospital room, with personnel constantly talking to and watching me, I felt more alone than ever. I was on medication and unable to talk or think clearly; I couldn't even walk without feeling faint. I had no peace, only pain. A fellow patient had loaned me a Bible just in case I wanted to read it. Out of desperation, I opened the Bible to a scripture I had learned as a child, the only one I could remember: Psalm 23.

"The Lord is my shepherd, I shall not want..." I cried as I read His Word. I knew Jesus loved me, but somehow I didn't believe it. Having nowhere else to turn and no other hope, I got on my knees beside my bed, looked up to the ceiling and cried, "Lord, if You're there, please help me!" I got into bed, sobbing, and felt a peace come over me that I couldn't explain. For the first time in many years, I slept soundly through the night.

When I awakened the next morning, I felt refreshed and renewed. I walked without assistance, I had energy; I made congenial conversation; and my mind was alert. The nurses asked what happened as they noticed that my eyes seemed brighter. During rounds the doctor also asked what had happened to me. The depression had been lifted! It was over! I knew I would be all right; I knew the Lord had worked a wonder in my life. It was at that time, in 1988, that I committed my life to Jesus. I truly *believed* in the love the Lord has for me.

I was discharged two days later. When I got home, I told everyone what had happened. I told them I knew the Lord had released me from the depression. I told them about the miracle God had done in my life. I believed that Jesus wanted me to be free. Even when I was so sick, when I couldn't even think by myself, He loved me and helped me.

In 1993, five years after His divine intervention, I began to feel burdened. Something was stealing my joy; I was slipping and sliding back into despair. With the enthusiastic encouragement of my sister, Clancy,* I agreed to attend a CLASS seminar led by Florence Littauer. Clancy had attended an earlier seminar led by the Littauers, and she seemed to have been changed for the better ever since. We planned our trip, packed the car and headed out. We were excited and expected a terrific time of fun and fellowship. The Lord blessed us with all of that — and so much more.

In my sorry state the first hours were awful, and the day was disastrous. I could feel the depression descending, and fear was in my heart. I was around Christians who didn't seem to have a care in the world; love for the Lord radiated from their faces. I focused on Jesus but still couldn't feel His love for me. I felt

* Not her real name

167

intimidated by all the Christians who could quote Scripture; they seemed so confident, and they reflected the love of the Lord. The more people I met and talked with, the more I wanted to run away. I didn't feel that I fit in, even in a small group. I kept trying to be unburdened; instead I felt weighed down. The messages that kept boggling my brain were declaring that I wasn't studious; I wasn't pretty; I laughed too loud; and I didn't say or do the right things. In short, they told me I shouldn't even be there. I loved Jesus, and I knew He had changed me in the past, but I needed to feel His love right then.

At the end of that first day, Clancy and I had an errand to do; it turned out to be a blessing in disguise. When we got into the car to begin a task that would take about three hours, I let loose and unbridled my feelings.

"I hate it here, and I never should have come!" I blurted out.

"Why do you say that? You have as much right to be here as anyone else does," Clancy stated.

"You just don't understand!" I yelled in frustration. "I just don't fit in here. Everyone is so spiritual; they can quote scripture from memory. I can't do that. They raise their hands and really love and worship the Lord; I want to join in, and I just can't seem to do it."

I went on and on about how I didn't belong there and how miserable I was. I told her my small group was filled with friendly folks who obviously felt the love of the Lord, but I already felt labeled as "one of those smokers" who had to sneak out between sessions for a smoke. Instead of getting some clarity from the seminar, I was more confused than before I came. Rather than feeling peaceful, I was in a panic. I didn't fit in with either the whole group or a smaller one. I didn't fit in at this conference. I didn't know what I was doing here! I wanted to go home, but I couldn't! I was stuck!

I didn't understand why Clancy even suggested that we come. And I sure didn't understand her response to my tirade. Clancy said simply, "Kathy, talk to Fred."

"I can't, Clancy. I just met the man. He certainly doesn't want to hear me complain about how miserable I am here. I'll just stay in our room until the conference is over."

"Kathy! Talk to Fred! He wants to know what's going on, and I know he can help you. Will you *please* talk to Fred!"

Clancy kept listening as I kept complaining. She kept telling me to talk to Fred. She assured me all the way back to the conference center that talking to Fred would help. After much argument, I agreed.

I didn't really want to see anyone, much less someone I had just met that day. After all, if Fred knew who I really was and if he knew about my background of depression and psychiatric treatments, he wouldn't like me either. I didn't want to admit to him that I hadn't memorized scripture verses; I figured he would think I wasn't spiritual or intelligent. If I had to admit to my insecurities and let him know how I really felt, he and Florence might think less of me.

Hesitantly, I asked Fred if I could see him. He agreed. When we met I talked openly and honestly about what was going on inside me. I was hurting, and I needed help. Fred asked me if I was willing to answer some questions. I agreed. The questions he asked helped free emotions that had been bottled up in me for years.

"Kathy, did you ever feel loved as a child?" Fred asked.

"I know my parents loved me," I replied logically. "They did all they knew how to do to help me. I was just a really rotten kid."

"I know that you *know* your parents loved you, but that's not what I asked," he said gently. "I asked you if you *felt loved* as a child."

I began crying as I remembered my feelings as a child. I had to answer, "No, I never felt loved."

I never felt loved by my family, nor did I feel loved by the Lord; I had done so many things wrong I didn't feel worthy of anyone's love. After more questions and prayer, Fred suggested there might be a reason why I felt this way. He asked me if I had ever been abused or rejected as a child. I told him I couldn't remember my early childhood, but I had always felt rejected and unacceptable; I still did.

Fred then showed me scripture verses assuring me of the Lord's help and healing. He emphasized that healing comes only from the hand of Jesus. Fred gave me a brief testimony of the healing the Lord had done in his life. As I listened, I felt renewed hope that God would do the same for me, hope that the healing God had done in my mind would also be done in my emotions. Fred went on to explain to me the value of written prayer, and he encouraged me to seek the Lord's counsel about finding the cause of my feelings. If the Lord led me to pray for healing of those deep hurts, Fred said he would pray with me.

The next day, while others were learning how to be speakers, I wrote a prayer for help and healing. Things came to my mind that I hadn't thought of for years. The last day of the conference the urge to pray was so strong that I couldn't wait. I sat down with Fred and Clancy for a time of prayer that was a turning point in my life.

I prayed that the Lord would minister to me in a way that would heal me of whatever was causing this chaos in my life and that He would help me understand His love. In prayer, the Lord brought back a memory. I saw a scene I hadn't seen before. I was in an upstairs room with my great-uncle. He was very dear to me; I loved him as much as I loved my father. But it was in that room that I relived the first horrible incident of sexual abuse at the hands of my great-uncle. While in prayer, I saw myself as I was then, a small, scared, three-year-old little girl. The pain was intense, and the anger profound. Hidden emotions hurled out of me. How could he do that? I was only three! What did I ever do to deserve that? I hated that man; I hated that room! I didn't ever want to go through that again. I felt beaten and broken. Why did it have to happen?

After I relived the memory, Fred suggested we continue in prayer.

"Kathy, would you be willing to allow the Lord to put you back in that room?" Fred asked.

Reluctantly, I agreed. Fred prayed that God would make that room a safe place, and he asked Him to heal me from this miserable memory. Fred prayed, and I was once again in that room, once again three years old. I was alone there, and I wasn't afraid.

I saw a brilliant light streaming in the window. As I turned to look into the light, I saw the Lord Jesus appear. He was standing there looking at me. There was such love in His eyes, such tenderness and understanding. His arms were reaching out to me as an invitation to come to Him. I actually heard Him say to me, "It's all right; you're safe. I am here with you. Come here to Me."

I went to Him, and He leaned down and picked me up in His arms. I hugged Him tightly.

I felt so safe with Him. I felt that I didn't have to be strong anymore; I could actually be a little girl around Him, one who enjoyed being cuddled and not criticized.

"You are My precious child," Jesus told me. "I love you very much. I have always loved you."

As He said those words I kept hugging Him. Nobody had ever called me *precious* before. I cried and told Him how sorry I was that I had done bad things with my great-uncle.

Jesus said, "It's not you who is to blame, precious Kathy. It was wrong of him to treat you that way. I know everything about you, and you are precious to Me. You always have been, and you always will be, My precious child. I love you."

When He put me down I had such a happy heart. He took my hand, and we walked out of that room and into the hallway. It was time to go.

"I am right here with you," He said to me as I looked up at Him.

I walked down the hallway and then turned back to look at Him one more time. I didn't want to leave. It was so wonderful to be in the presence of the Lord. Still, I knew it was time.

Jesus said to me, "I am still here. I will always be right here."

The whole time I was in prayer, I had been describing to Fred my memory and my experience with Jesus. Now I was sobbing with hurt, relief and gratitude.

Then Fred asked me, "Kathy, which of your hands was Jesus holding?"

"He was holding my left hand," I replied.

"Which hand was He holding yours with?" Fred continued.

"He was holding me with His right hand."

Then Fred said, "He was holding you in His right hand. You were at the right hand of Jesus."

"Yes, I was!" I realized the full impact of being in the right hand of my Lord and Savior.

Our prayer time was over, but my healing journey had just begun. I was so thankful for the blessing Jesus gave me. Although I hadn't told anyone, I remembered the dream I had long ago of devoting my life to His work. Now that dream was alive again! I wanted to see Him and talk with Him forever. I felt refreshed, restored and renewed in Him and His love. I now *felt,* for the first time in my life, the love Jesus has for me.

Clancy and I went out of the building and into the beautiful, warm sunshine. When we sat down on a bench facing the bay, I suddenly began to shake. Without warning I was trembling from the top of my head to the soles of my feet. I had suffered anxiety attacks before, but this was different. I looked to heaven and asked the Lord to continue His mighty work in me; Clancy held my hand and prayed along with me. I knew the Lord was cleansing me and filling me with His Spirit. A new awareness of the goodness and glory of God filled my soul in such a way that I can't even describe it. I knew my Savior and Lord had claimed me as His own!

Later that same year, I attended a Promise of Healing workshop. I had mixed feelings about attending: I was excited about more healing, but I was frightened that more discoveries would bring back the depression. I prayed the Lord would continue the work He had begun and calm my fears. He did all of that — and more!

At the seminar, another whole part emerged, an angry, bitter, resentful personality. I felt an anger I hadn't felt since I was eight years old when I became so enraged that I put my fist through a window. The speakers at the workshop stirred up anger, and my joy was gone. I was defiant and defensive. I didn't like this at all, and I wasn't sure if I wanted to know about any more abuse. I was hurting, and I knew I needed to pray.

I prayed into the presence of the Lord with a prayer counselor and with Clancy as my prayer partner. God brought me to another childhood home. I remembered the outside of this house but had no recollection of the rooms inside. I was at the top of the driveway just staring at the house; I didn't want to go inside. I was afraid of that house. There was something about that house I didn't want to face.

But Clancy was strongly urging me to go into the house; she said I had to go. She knew the childhood pain that would be revealed behind that door — because she lived through it with me. I prayed that Jesus would give me strength, courage and further healing. I found myself inside the house looking at a little girl who was sitting in the upstairs hallway outside a closed door. It was confusing to me because I was watching the child, but the child was *me*. I was that little, broken, five-year-old girl sitting forlornly in the hallway; but at the same time I was the angry, strong, grown woman who was watching! I always knew I had more than one personality, but nobody else had known it. I had personalities to deal with every situation; it was the only way I could survive! The Lord was showing me so clearly that He knew all about me, even my deepest secrets.

The Lord showed me why little Kathy was waiting outside the closed door. It would soon be my turn with the great-uncle. My sister was in there with him now; my turn would be next. When the call came, little Kathy got up, reached for the doorknob and opened the door. Great-uncle was waiting.

During this memory I kept switching personalities. When I could withstand the hurt, I was little Kathy. When the pain was too much, I switched back to a grown adult. Even though I had lived through this awful abuse, the pain was still too intense to bear.

After the ordeal in that room was over, little Kathy left the room, leaving the door open. I looked back and saw a bright light. I stared into it, knowing Jesus would come to me. Out of a corner of that room He moved toward me. I was no longer alone.

173

He picked me up in His arms and held me close while I cried.

"My sweet child, you are so precious to Me. I know all that you have gone through," Jesus said. "I'm sorry he hurt you, but you are clean now. I will take the pain away and heal you. Though you have gone through much suffering I will turn it to good. Trust Me."

As little Kathy kept clinging to Jesus, I watched. Both as a young child and as a grownup, I wanted to stay close to Him and never let go. As He was holding little Kathy He held out His other arm, inviting the grown-up me to come to Him.

When I approached, He held little Kathy in one arm and hugged grown-up me in the other. As He hugged us close to Him, He brought us closer and closer to each other. I reached out and hugged little Kathy. Jesus hugged us so tightly that little Kathy and grown-up me became one. I looked at Jesus in awe that He knew me so well and could heal me in such a wonderful way.

Then He said, "I told you before that I am always here. I have always been right here, and I always will be. I know everything about you, and I chose you to be Mine. I will restore you to become who I created you to be."

I kept asking the Lord to forgive me; I felt so dirty and ashamed. Anger consumed my soul and interfered in all I said and did. His answer was forgiveness — forgiveness for the one who had betrayed and abused me.

The Lord told me, "Just as I have forgiven you for your sins, you must forgive your great-uncle."

I was unable and unwilling to even think about it. I was hurt, and I wanted my great-uncle to hurt too — even more. I told the Lord I just couldn't do it; I just couldn't forgive that man for what he did to me and my sister.

Jesus continued, "You must forgive him. I will change your heart and teach you how. I know you can't forgive him on your own, but I will help you. Without forgiveness, you will always be burdened. It is up to you to forgive your great-uncle; his judgment will come."

My heart was immediately softened toward my great-uncle. Rather than hating him, I hurt for him. I don't know whether or not he ever became a Christian, but he will have to answer for his actions.

Before our prayer ended, Jesus said to me, "Remember, I will always be right here."

I felt lighter and freer than I'd ever felt before. It was then that I came to understand that my complete healing would be a journey, not an event.

It's incredible what the Lord does and how He does it. Even when I was broken and had so many parts (though I still hadn't told anyone), God used me. During that conference I met people in the parking lot (the smoking area), where we would fellowship and pray together.

After the conference was over Clancy and I took off for a couple days' rest and relaxation. We went to a cousin's house some distance away. During this time my smoking habit was weighing heavily upon my heart. I wanted to grow closer and closer to Jesus. I didn't want anything at all to come between us, including my smoking. I didn't know if this was an issue or not. I knew He loved me and I loved Him no matter what; after all, He knew everything about me, and He still loved me. Still, I needed to know.

The next morning I woke up, put on my bathrobe, grabbed my cigarettes and went outside for my usual "morning thing" of drinking coffee and smoking. I was enjoying myself. Then the burden clouded my heart. I looked up to heaven and said, "Lord, if my smoking is an issue, please let me know; I don't want anything between us. But, Lord, let me know in such a way that I cannot mistake it for something else or rationalize it. Thank You, Father."

I finished my cigarette, opened the door and headed toward the kitchen. I was only halfway there when I felt so dizzy I could barely walk. I was so faint and nauseous by the time I got to the kitchen, I had to sit down and lower my head to my knees. My cousin and my sister saw me, reached out to help and asked with great concern, "Kathy, are you OK?"

I knew what had happened. I lifted my head, looked at them and said, "I am not supposed to be smoking any more!"

I told them what I had asked the Lord to do, and I asked them to agree with me in prayer that the Lord would take away the craving and desire to smoke. When we joined hands and came to the Lord with our petition, I knew my prayer had already been answered. I continue to praise my Lord Jesus for this mighty miracle. Since that moment, the smell of smoke has sickened me, and I have never had a desire to smoke again.

Since the Lord revealed to me His knowledge of my many personalities (parts), it had been heavy on my heart to come to Him and receive more healing. One night I had two lengthy prayer sessions: one with Fred and one with Clancy. While I was in prayer with Fred, more miraculous healing took place as the Lord merged two quiet, hurting little Kathys into me. But God wasn't finished — not even then. After my prayer session with Fred, I called Clancy to share with her what had happened. I told her that I knew there was something more.

"Do you want to pray?" Clancy asked.

"I just did pray — with Fred," I replied. "But something is still going on."

Clancy repeated, "Do you want to pray?"

"I don't know what's going on, Clancy. I still feel as though something is happening, and I'm really getting ticked off about it."

"Do you want to pray?" she repeated with urgency.

I agreed. During a prayer session that lasted three hours, I came face-to-face with a part of me I had seen when I prayed with Clancy in California, a personality I didn't like and didn't want to deal with, a part that I tried to hide away and hide behind — the angry one. This personality was so enraged there was no room for love. Only bitterness, self-hatred, contempt and condemnation could abide in this part.

The Lord continued His mighty ministry in me. As we prayed I again came into the presence of the Lord. He took me back to that same horrid house, that same horrible room. There I saw more abuse. This time my sister was the victim. Upon seeing her suffer, the angry personality emerged in full force. This new little Kathy was enraged. This part was filled with such fury she couldn't contain it. Little Kathy marched up to the bed and stomped her feet!

"Leave her alone! Don't do that to my sister! Get away from her!" I screamed at the top of my lungs at my great-uncle.

He stopped what he was doing to my sister, and she scampered off the bed into the corner. He turned to me, picked me up and dumped me onto the bed.

"OK, I'll leave her alone. I'll use you instead — for all of it."

And he did. When he was finished, he left the room and I, as the little girl, sat up, sobbing on the bed. Clancy was sitting in the corner, scared, and she was sobbing too. She had seen what had happened to me. After that I alone got the abuse from my great-uncle and from his friends as well. Everyone thought my sister was the strong one. Everyone thought she protected and took care of me. Instead I suffered the abuse to save her. I was enraged at the injustice as well as the abuse.

Then I saw that same magnificent light coming through the window. In its midst the Lord again revealed Himself. I angrily went to Jesus, and He said, "My dearest Kathy, I know all about it. I know you're angry, and I know why. You're angry with Me, and I know that, too. I love you. You're safe. Be angry, but don't sin. Voice your anger, and then give it to Me."

I did voice it. I cried. I yelled. I screamed. I ranted and raved at my sister and at the Lord. For over two hours that night, my poisonous feelings of abandonment, injustice, bitterness and hatred exploded from my body and mind. Every bit of anger came out of me. The Lord allowed me to be freed from that rage that had kept me in bondage for most of my life.

Finally I was spent. My anger was over, but the pain was overwhelming. Then peace began to flow through me; I thought my healing session was finished. But the Lord knew better.

While still standing beside Him, I had feelings of joy and expectancy, though for what I didn't know. Suddenly, through the door came many little Kathys. They came from everywhere:

around the corner, under the bed, behind the door. They were no longer afraid to be one with me. The little one who I knew was the heart of me came running around the corner grinning and giggling, then she skipped *into* me. We were one. I hugged every little personality as each one came to me. One by one the Lord hugged them all into me, eighteen during that prayer session. For the first time I felt safe, secure and sound. I then asked the Lord to give me rest and restore my strength.

We continued in prayer. Suddenly I found myself on a lovely hillside standing before a beautiful shade tree. The grass was green and lush, and majestic mountains could be seen in the distance. Standing under the tree facing me was the Lord Jesus. I bowed down to give Him praise and thanks for all He is and all He has done. He touched the top of my head and said, "You are Mine. I have chosen you, and I know you by name. You are My child, and I want you to come to Me freely about anything. I am always here for you."

He put a garment around my shoulders and fastened it under my chin. It was a big, bright, beautiful cape woven with threads of fuschia and purple with gold and silver sparkles all over it. It was splendid. I danced and twirled around and watched as it glittered and glistened in the bright sunshine. Then I looked at Him in amazement and wondered what I had ever done to merit such a gift. I had done nothing; He had done it all.

"Jesus, why did You give me this beautiful cape?" I asked.

Jesus said to me, "This is just for you. I have given you this robe and fastened it onto you so no one can take it away. You are special. You are Mine. You are My precious child. I have claimed you, I have cleansed you, and I have dressed you in My robe of righteousness. This is part of you. Don't ever forget your robe. If you ever doubt My love, look at it closely and remember."

Never had I experienced such joy in all my life as I did that night. Never did I dream I would have such wonderful miracles happen to me. I felt so cherished, so comforted, so protected and so loved.

I asked the Lord if we were finished.

He replied, "We're done for now, but there's more to do. Trust Me; I will restore you."

The Lord has reunited into me a total of twenty-six different personalities. The voices are stilled, my mind is mended and my soul is serene. The Master's touch has healed me and made me whole. Each day I put on the robe of righteousness along with the full armor of God; I never leave home without them. Since the Lord has restored me to what He created me to be, He has used me to help others receive the same kind of healing that comes only from Him.

I discovered that the Lord had brought healing to Clancy before my own healing. She had been praying for me and believing that God would provide an opportunity for my healing. Now we can share the miracle gift of seeing Jesus with each other.

The Lord's help and healing continue in my life. He has broken bondages and delivered me from darkness. He has taken my burdens and given me His blessings. His hand on my life is something I long for and look for. I am on a journey with Jesus, a journey that will lead me home.[1]

Does Kathy's healing sound like a miracle to you? From the average person's perspective this is truly a miracle, an extraordinary event for which there is no human or logical explanation. From our position as Christians it is simply a part of the glorious inheritance available to each one of us in Christ Jesus.

We hesitate to call the Lord's work in Kathy a miracle but instead recognize it as an awesome, wondrous joy to behold. Best of all, such healing is available to every Christian in need who is willing to come to Him. He proclaimed in Matthew 11:28, "Come to Me, all who are weary and heavy-laden, and I will give you rest." Kathy came to Him, and He gave her that rest — perfect inner peace.

Today Kathy is speaking out publicly on her trauma and on the healing the Lord has done in her life. She spends hours upon hours each week praying with others, both in person and by telephone, that they too might receive the same comfort she has received. She is a living example of believing and acting upon the truth of 2 Corinthians 1:3-4, that the "God of all comfort...comforts us in all our affliction so that we may be able to comfort those who are in any affliction with the comfort with which we ourselves are comforted of God."

18

Be Watchful, Be Vigilant

ONE OF THE best kept secrets in Christendom is that you and I, because we are Christians, have power and authority over satan. Survey twenty Christians, asking each one individually, "Do you believe in the existence of satan or the devil?" Chances are that nineteen will give you an unequivocal yes, and the twentieth will probably acknowledge his existence but not quite so certainly.

Ask, "Do you know he has power?" and once again you will undoubtedly receive affirmation and agreement.

Next ask, "Do you think he uses or is able to use that power against you?" Now you will probably run into significant doubt and uncertainty in the answers you receive.

And then, "Do you think you as an individual have power and authority that exceeds his?" Now the indecision will run deeper!

Finally, ask, "Do you know how to use your authority over him? Have you ever used it?" Many will respond no. After all, if

Christians do not really know that satan can attack, interfere with and influence them, there is no reason for them to know how to deal with him. He is, for many, a non-issue!

The simple truth is that satan — the prince of darkness, lucifer, the devil, apollyon, abaddon or baal, whatever name may be most familiar — has already exerted his controlling influence over many unsuspecting Christians. As a result they are spiritually powerless, ineffective and often defeated.

> Be on the alert. Your adversary, the devil, prowls about like a roaring lion, seeking someone to devour. But resist him, firm in your faith (1 Pet. 5:8-9).

It need not be so! We have nothing to fear in satan! Fear comes only when we become slothful and lazy. The Lord Jesus has already given us His power and authority over satan. A foe he is, but he has already been defeated. It remains for us only to exercise the power that is ours by inheritance. Why fear someone over whom you can have immediate control and supremacy? We fear the unknown or the danger confronting us only when we see no alternative or escape. With satan we do not need an escape! We can move in with confidence and clear him out. He is the one who must run. When we move forward against him with determination, poise and conviction, he will flee!

The Word of God gives us all the knowledge we need. "Resist the devil and *he will flee from you!*"[1] He has no choice. He must flee when we use the spiritual weapons the Lord has already given us. Did the Lord Jesus ever run from the devil or evil spirits? Of course not! Jesus met them head-on and exercised His authority over them, and they obeyed!

Likewise, when we invoke the power Jesus has given us, satan and those who serve him must obey us.

God's Armory

Listen to what God says to us in 2 Corinthians 10:3-6 (NIV):

1. "For though we live in the world, we do not wage war as the world does."

2. "The weapons we fight with are not the weapons of the world."

3. "On the contrary, they have divine power to demolish strongholds."

4. "We demolish arguments and every pretension that sets itself up against the knowledge of God."

5. "We take captive every thought to make it obedient to Christ."

6. "We will be ready to punish every act of disobedience."

We can glean several insights from this forthright proclamation of the weapons in God's armory.

Line 1: We do not wage war as the world wages war. We already know the outcome; we know who will be the victor. There is no mystery!

Line 2: We have many different weapons available to us, each designed to be uniquely successful in specific situations; we need not use the same weapon for every conflict. Our weapons are not worldly. They do not have to be fired, swung or transported. They require neither basic nor advanced training. We need to know only what weapons are available to us and then go into God's armory to get them.

Line 3: Our weapons have divine power to demolish and destroy strongholds and fortresses the enemy may have erected. These weapons have *power to destroy!* The issue is never in doubt.

Line 4: We will demolish everything the enemy sets up against the knowledge and the truth of God.

Line 5: We are fully armed and equipped spiritually to take captive all servants of the enemy commanding that they become obedient to Christ or suffer the dire consequences of utter defeat.

Line 6: We do not threaten. We are ready, and we *will*, without any hesitation, punish all disobedience!

Our Most Important Weapon

The most valuable and important weapon God has placed in His armory is too seldom used, and for many it lies rusty and neglected. That is the weapon of rebuking, binding and banishing satan. How often do you personally exercise your God-given authority over satan? If you're like most Christians, you seldom, if ever, use this powerful weapon. You will be thrilled and strengthened at the changes that will take place in your life when you begin to throw your spiritual weight and authority around!

First Peter 5:8-9 tells us, "Be on the alert. Your adversary, the devil, prowls about like a roaring lion, seeking someone to devour. But resist him, firm in your faith." If the Scripture says it so succinctly, why do so many Christians ignore the fact that satan is boldly seeking to devour anyone he can? Though he prowls about like a roaring lion, he is actually a cowardly pussy-cat who slinks off into the bulrushes when confronted with strength and authority in the name of the Lord Jesus Christ.

At the same time, satan is also a subtle infiltrator (see Gen. 3:1). He strikes when and where we least expect him. Is that a surprise? He is a liar and deceiver. He doesn't fight fair. That is why we must be alert and vigilant. We must learn to discern and identify his attacks and interferences for what they are.

Paul told the Corinthians, "I fear...as the serpent beguiled Eve through his subtility, so your minds should be corrupted."[2] "And no wonder, for even satan disguises himself as an angel of light. Therefore it is not surprising if his servants also disguise themselves as servants of righteousness."[3] Scripture, both the New Testament and the Old, is replete with illustrations, admonitions and descriptions exhorting us to be alert. Yet much of the church remains asleep and unaware or, too often, disinterested.

The Authority for Using Our Weapon

Let us look briefly at a few key scriptures.

184

1. "Then he called his twelve disciples together, and gave them power and authority over all devils."[4]

Here a gift has been given to the twelve. They have received power and authority over all devils.

2. "After this the Lord chose another seventy-two men[5] and sent them out, two by two, to go ahead of him to every town and place where he himself was about to go...the seventy-two men came back in great joy. 'Lord,' they said, 'even the demons obeyed us when we commanded them in your name!'"[6]

Clearly these seventy-two appointees have been given the identical power and authority that was given to the twelve! The gift is no longer limited in scope or bestowal! The Lord has chosen to give it to this additional larger, unnamed, unidentified and apparently insignificant group.

3. Then Jesus replied to them, "Behold, I give unto you power to tread on serpents [metaphorically satan] and scorpions [evil spirits], and over all the power of the enemy: and nothing shall by any means hurt you...the spirits are subject unto you."[7]

Read that last verse again. It is an amazing empowerment that is often overlooked. Simply stated, you and I as Christians have already been given Jesus' power over satan, demonic forces, evil spirits and over "all the power of the enemy." The verse also states that, even though satan has power, we have power *over* his power! Our power is greater than his power, and therefore he is subject to our power when we exercise it. Hence when we read in James 4:7 to "resist the devil," we are also told, "he will flee from you." He has no choice. He must flee. The roaring lion will slink off into the bulrushes like a whipped pussy cat.

The One Absolute Essential

In our own name or in our own power we have absolutely no authority or power over satan. In fact, if we try to battle him he will laugh and sneer at us and attack us with even more determination because he knows we are not armed. He will see that we are defenseless.

But the moment we invoke Jesus' power, satan becomes defenseless. The power is seen in Luke 10:17: "Lord, even the demons are subject to us *in Your name.*" When you speak to satan or his servants, when you command them in the name of the Lord Jesus Christ, they have no choice but to obey! Try it. If you have never exercised your authority over satan before, you will be amazed at how quickly he flees.

For two reasons, taking authority over satan should always be done aloud. First, Jesus always spoke aloud to him, never silently or under His breath. Scripture records that demons and evil spirits responded to Jesus' audible commands. Second, there seems to be no evidence that satan can read our minds, but there is certain proof that he can hear us. The loudness of your voice is inconsequential. In other words, your authority is not enhanced by shouting. Jesus never did. He simply spoke with authority. You and I can do exactly the same. Our complete and only authority rests in His name!

A Suggested Prayer

Following is a simple but effective prayer for rebuking satan. It will be reprinted in large bold letters in the appendix for you to remove, copy and place in strategic places in your home and/or workplace to use until you become so familiar with it you can recite it from memory. For your own benefit, it is recommended that you stand when rebuking satan. Standing will help you comprehend that you are actually commanding him to obey you. Furthermore, Ephesians 6:12 tells us to "stand" against him.

May I invite you to actually stand up now and read the following commandment prayer aloud. Speak clearly with God-given authority in your voice, but do not shout:

> **In the name of the Lord Jesus Christ,**
> **I take authority over you, satan!**
> **I rebuke you, I bind you, I banish you!**
> **I command you to leave this place.**
> **I command you to leave me.**
> **You are not permitted to interfere in my life.**
> **In the name of the Lord Jesus Christ, satan,**
> **I tell you and all your evil spirits to be gone!**
> **Be gone from here!**

Then raise your hands and look up to Jesus who gave you this power and authority. Thank Him aloud using your own words or the following prayer.

> Lord Jesus, I thank You for the power You have given me over satan. I thank You that he must obey me. I thank You for the freedom You have given me. Now, dear Lord, I ask that You fill me with your Holy Spirit; fill me, Lord, and give me your perfect peace. Lord Jesus, I thank You, I praise You, I worship You. Amen.

As you stand and read aloud the commandment prayer and the prayer of thankfulness, something very significant and discernible may happen. If any emotional struggles were going on within you such as fear, depression, anger or low self-worth, to name just a few, you will very likely feel that they have lifted or completely disappeared! Why? Because they were simply an attack of the enemy. You have commanded the attacker to leave you. It does not mean that he will not attack again tomorrow. But if he does, you will know how to rebuke him and to resist and "extinguish all the flaming missiles of the evil one."[8]

In the suggested commandment prayer only eight words are absolutely essential. Otherwise you can modify it in any way you feel led by the Spirit to fit your circumstances and need. What are those eight essential words? Repeat them now aloud:

"In the name of the Lord Jesus Christ!"

I am convinced that the enemy knows all our weaknesses, our vulnerabilities or, as I call them, our "open windows." He never attacks us in our area of strengths. He attacks only our frailties, especially areas where he has built strongholds and fortresses of the mind.

Long-term freedom from his attacks involves several additional things. First it requires that we find the open windows and shut them. It also requires daily specific prayer for the cleansing and healing of these areas. It requires daily rebuking of the enemy, casting him out of your home, your life and your ministry. It requires your feeling absolutely assured that you do have authority over him and that you have no hesitation to use that power against him!

Some time ago during my daily prayer time (I call it my daily communion with my Lord), I was clearly directed by the Lord to automatically and regularly rebuke the enemy whether or not I felt attacked. For some reason which I cannot specifically explain, I did this only periodically despite the Lord's direction. I did do it consistently when I felt or knew I was being attacked, and when I perceived any emotional disruption in the promised peace of Jesus.[9] Whenever I did so the bondage, or whatever it was, lifted immediately. The feeling of release is always clear evidence that you were experiencing an attack! And I did pray regularly for discernment so I would quickly recognize any momentary upset or disharmony for what it really was and take the necessary rapid and appropriate response against it.

About two months ago, however, as I was communing with the Lord, He reminded me that He had already directed me to stand against the enemy *daily,* whether or not I thought I was being attacked. I knew I had been gently reprimanded, and this time I took the admonition to heart! Without missing a day, I have stood against the enemy since then. I have banished him from my life, from my wife's life, from the ministries the Lord has given us, from my children's and grandchildren's lives. I wish I could fully describe to you what a change this has made. I wish I could tell you how free from attack both Florence and I have been! I have long recognized that I am the spiritual head of my wife,[10] and therefore I believe it is my scriptural duty to protect her in every way, emotionally, physically and by all means spiritually. By banishing satan from my wife and by standing in front of her with my shield of faith in one hand and my sword in the other, I am fulfilling my scriptural responsibility.

What a change it has made! It has been *incredible.* There have been no attacks; the windows of vulnerabilities and compulsions the enemy opened in me many years ago have been securely shut and sealed. He has not succeeded in opening any at all that I am aware of. Likewise, things that once might have bothered Florence and caused consternation for her no longer do! Despite the stresses and rigors of her life of ministry and travel, she now sleeps more soundly than she ever has before!

I will continue my daily banishing and bashing of the enemy until the Lord tells me it is no longer necessary. I have a feeling I may be waiting for that message a long time! Why do I share this with you? Because I strongly encourage you to do the same thing. *Banish satan daily from your life.* You will be just as thrilled with the results as I have been. A good time to do it is just before you go to sleep. The enemy loves to interfere with your sleep.

Remember eight-year-old Bradley whose story I shared with you in chapter 15? I taught him to rebuke and banish satan. When he did he slept through the night, completely free of the bad dreams about monstrous spiders. When he got careless and stopped for a while, the nightmares came back!

You have the sample prayer commanding satan to be gone. As the Scripture says, "Now you know this truth; how happy you will be if you put it into practice!"[11] I urge you to photocopy the prayer as it appears in the appendix and place the copies in strategic places as reminders to exercise daily your authority over satan and over all the powers of the enemy.

It is the same prayer we always pray when we are praying someone into the presence of the Lord. This prayer is definitive and final, so we can proceed without his interference. Having said it, you have effectively banished satan in the name of the Lord Jesus Christ!

Remember, the Bible admonishes us to, "Be watchful, be vigilant"!

Breaking Strongholds

We have just seen that the weapons with which we fight have the divine power to demolish strongholds, or fortresses, of the mind. What is a stronghold? A stronghold is sometimes referred to as a soul tie. The two are similar, but there are some differences.

A stronghold may be defined as any beachhead that satan has secured in your mind that holds you in some form of bondage, or captivity, from which you seem to be unable to escape. A stronghold tends to focus on a place or a thing; it may be characterized by:

- Any form of obsession or compulsion.

- Any deviant behavior or activity that you know is displeasing to the Lord or guilt-producing in yourself.

- Any place you find yourself going to, either physically or mentally, that causes you distress.

- Disturbing pictures that frequently or occasionally cross your mind's eye.

- Voices in your head that say you are stupid or worthless.

- Any form of shame that lingers and resists prayer and confession.

- Anger, bitterness, jealousy or unforgiveness that you cannot or do not want to release.

- Lingering dreams that cause distress and anxiety.

- Worry, fear, depression or panic attacks.

A soul tie may be described as any illegal or inappropriate emotional or spiritual bonding with another person. The focus of a soul tie is some form of unacceptable human relationship; it may be characterized by:

- Any illegal sexual relationship, including but not limited to, those formed as a result of childhood sexual abuse or interference in childhood or adult years.

- Any illegal or inappropriate bonding relationship with another (mother or father, counselor or counselee, pastor or other strong, controlling person).

- Someone you have dreams about or wake up in the night thinking about.

- Someone your mind continues to focus on, especially obsessively.

- Continuing emotional reaction to another individual when you meet him or her unexpectedly, hear his or her voice on the phone or hear his or her name mentioned.

- Someone of whom you may be emotionally afraid.

- Someone whose name or face comes into your mind while you are intimate with your spouse.

- Someone you dread running into or hope you won't see.

- Someone you bond with in ministry who meets or feeds your unfilled emotional needs.

How do we break a stronghold or a soul tie?

First, we must acknowledge its existence and be willing to name it.

Second, we must recognize that it is damaging our life and internal harmony.

Third, we must determine that we will be freed of it totally, completely and eternally.

Fourth, we must be willing and committed to take whatever

steps are necessary to break or destroy it.

Fifth, we must take out a specific prayer from God's armory and wield it as a weapon with no mercy for the offender. The following prayer can help you break free of the strongholds and soul ties satan may try to establish in your mind. Select (a) the phrases to pray about strongholds or (b) the phrases to pray about soul ties.

> Dear Lord Jesus, I confess
>
> (a) The existence of _____, a stronghold upon my life,
>
> (or)
>
> (b) That my relationship with _____ is sinful,
>
> and I repent of it. I ask You, O Lord, to cleanse me of this unrighteousness.
>
> In the name of the Lord Jesus Christ, I place the cross of Christ between satan and me, and I declare
>
> (a) the stronghold of _____
>
> (or)
>
> (b) the soul tie with _____
>
> to be null and void. I am cleansed by the blood of the Lord Jesus Christ, and satan, I command you to release each and every hold that you have on me.
>
> I thank You, my Lord and my God, for the power that You have given to me to break all the bondages that satan has attempted to place on me. Amen.

This prayer of spiritual authority should be repeated individually for each stronghold or soul tie you can identify. Pray this prayer as soon as you recognize the existence or possibility of a stronghold or soul tie. Remember, there is no such thing as praying too much! You make no mistake if you pray against a condition you suspect but are not sure of. The Lord loves prayer, and satan hates it. It's that simple!

One pastor who attended one of our Promise of Healing workshops told me later that when it was over he went home and made a list of everyone to whom he suspected he had a soul tie from any point in his life. He then prayed the prayer outlined above with each one. It took a full two hours. When he was done he said he had never felt so free in his entire life!

Recently, a dear friend, a mature Christian woman, shared with my wife that she was having troublesome dreams involving her teenage sweetheart who had had an affair with one of her older relatives. This affair not only destroyed their teenage romance but caused her to feel for much of her life that she had been abandoned and cast aside by one man after another. In addition, she was still struggling with anger and with feelings of being controlled by that older female relative!

The next day we met with the woman and prayed the prayer of authority to break the soul ties with both the old boyfriend and the female relative. Then we prayed again, and I asked the Lord Jesus to come to her and to minister to her regarding the feelings of worthlessness and abandonment. He did come to her. She saw a seventeen-year-old girl standing next to Jesus. It was her teenage self that had been so devastated by the affair.

Not only did Jesus reunite her two personalities, He turned the woman around and held her from behind with His arms securely around her. He said, "Together we will the face the future. You will no longer be alone." Afterward, she said to me, "I didn't lose any weight, but I feel so much lighter!" The Lord Jesus gave her the weapons to break the soul ties and ministered personally to her remaining deep hurts. The dreams disappeared, and she no longer fears the relative. She too has been touched by the Master!

19

More
Wondrous Works

The Lord Jesus continues to show us and teach us the wonderful and gentle ways He will heal many kinds of hurts and encumbrances that are weighing down so many of His children.

In the past five years there has been a sharp rise in the number of women who are confessing to deep guilt and emotional pain due to abortions they endured fifteen or twenty years earlier when they were told their choice was nothing more than a simple medical procedure with no harmful aftereffects. Now, years later, they are finding out that what they were told then was not the truth. There is often a great deal of delayed anguish resulting from abortions.

However, the Lord has shown us that He will take away the shame and the depression. He will forgive. He will allow the mother to see that the child is safely and happily in heaven with Him. How can we actually know this? Is it possible to see an unborn child? If we ask, He is faithful and just, and He will reveal Himself and the child that was previously thought to be lost. Imagine the incomprehensible comfort to a mother to find that her child actually lives and was never lost at all. Perhaps what was really lost was her opportunity to be that child's guardian for a period of time. The healing and cleansing by the Lord of post-abortion stress syndrome, as it is sometimes called, is something He is showing us over and over again.

One person who struggled for many years with the pain and guilt of abortion was Fran,* who met us at a women's conference in the Midwest. Fran had struggled for many years as a result of the counseling she had received and the decision she had made because of it. After our time of prayer ministry, Fran wrote this report and has agreed to let me include it in this book so she can share her experience with you.

> My heart had been hurting for a long, long time over an abortion I had in the early eighties. For years I'd been torn with anguish. I couldn't bear to look at any literature, TV shows or documentaries about abortion without reacting emotionally. My eyes would fill with tears, and I couldn't wash away the lump in my throat. I was totally unable to talk about it to anyone, especially those I felt close to. I was so deeply ashamed of myself for ever doing such a horrible thing. Often I couldn't even look at myself in the mirror without disgust. I shared my shame with very few others, and even those few were too many for me. I cringed at the thought of anyone knowing what I had done.
>
> I thought that I had resolved these feelings a few years ago, but lately they had been pressing in on me again, leaving me with a very heavy heart. My husband seemed to have settled it in his heart and mind; he seemed OK with it. But inner peace eluded me. I knew the time had finally come for me to deal with

* Not her real name

my guilt and pain once and for all.

After the conference I spoke with Fred and asked him if I could make an appointment to work on something that had been bothering me a great deal. He was willing, and we set the time for Thursday night of the following week.

When Thursday night came, Fred asked me what was weighing so heavily on me. I told him about the abortion and explained that my heart had been breaking ever since. I told him I felt that I was worthless for ever having gone through with it.

Fred reassured me that Jesus knew my heart, that He knew how sorry I was and that He had already forgiven me. My problem was forgiving myself!

I told Fred I had often wondered what that child would be like today. He asked me if I would like to know where my baby was, and then he asked, "Would you like to see it?" I wasn't totally shocked at his question because I had spoken to him before and knew that the Lord was using him to help hurting women like me. If this were possible, yes, I would like to see my baby. I wanted to know where he or she was. I wanted any information I could get about my baby.

Fred asked me to pray and simply tell the Lord what was on my heart and what I wanted to know. He said he would pray after I did. I went to the Lord in prayer. This was difficult for me because I felt too undeserving to even consider asking Him for help. My heart was so full I couldn't get the words out easily. When I finished, Fred prayed. As he was praying, I felt a softness (the only way I know to describe it) surround me and a sweet kind of peacefulness envelop me.

As the feeling settled over me, I saw someone holding an infant in His arms. I knew that someone was Jesus. I could feel the love flowing from Him to this child. Tears flowed down my cheeks, and my throat seemed to be closed so tightly that I had a difficult time speaking. I was in awe of what I was experiencing.

I knew without any doubt that this child was my own baby and that it was being cradled in the loving arms of Jesus. As I looked more closely I realized that it was a little girl, and the name Bethany came to me. I knew that was her name. As I gazed at them, the child reached out a tiny hand and touched the cheek of Jesus. I told Fred what I was seeing, and I heard him say, "Praise God."

Fred asked me if I wanted to say anything to Bethany. I did want to, and I wanted to hold her myself. I was standing right there in the presence of Jesus, and He held her out to me to hold in my own arms. I held her close to my heart and whispered in her ear that I loved her. I told her I was so sorry. I asked if she could please forgive me. Above all I needed to let her know she was not rejected and that she was loved.

Fred said I could hold her for as long as I wished, but at some point I would have to let her go. The assurance I had received from Jesus filled me with calmness, and I knew then that I would be able to release her to Him. She would be in His safe hands.

I didn't want to let go of her, but at some point I must have, because I realized she was no longer an infant but a little girl about eleven or twelve years old. She appeared to be very happy and content and at peace with her surroundings. Then I knew everything was all right.

During this time I felt great pain at first, then complete peace. The Lord Jesus' healing touch filled me with a peace I had not known since the early eighties. Our Lord's tender mercy is so awesome, and I am so thankful that He gave me the assurance I needed and filled me with peace. Thank You, Jesus.

While abortion is very wrong, our Lord Jesus does forgive, and He does not want us to go on beating ourselves up over it. He heals and forgives and wants us to help others who have been in the same position we were. With God's help, I will.[1]

Florence and I have never had to face this kind of emotional trauma, but as many of our friends know, we lost two infant boys. Both appeared to be normal and healthy when they were born. Around the age of six or seven months, however, each one showed signs of the slowing of natural growth. Examination of and later exploratory surgery on the second son indicated a failure of the brain to develop in a natural and healthy manner. Before their first birthdays, both boys had lost all of their normal faculties. Our first son, little Freddie, died at the age of two. One week later we learned that his brother, Larry, had the same malady. Larry lived for the remainder of his life in a private nursing home as a living vegetable. He died at the age of nineteen at the same physical size he had been at the age of one! He never grew or developed. Yes, we have known hurt and tragedy ourselves.

Today, however, both through the Scriptures and the joy the Lord has given us many times over of seeing mothers momentarily reunited in the spirit with their long lost babies, we have the peace and the certainty of knowing that our boys also have a new body, incorruptible and spiritual.[2] We know that they, too, are safely and securely in heaven with their Lord Jesus.

Two at One Time

"The effectual fervent prayer of a righteous man availeth much." Most of us are familiar with this passage from the King James Version of James 5:16, but we may not fully understand how effectual our prayers can be! Of one thing we can be absolutely certain: our prayers are always heard. Further, we can believe that when the Lord said in John 14:14, "If ye shall ask any thing in my name, I will do it" (KJV), He meant it. Yes, we can accept that our prayers are heard and that when we ask according to His will He will do what we ask.

Sometimes we are privileged to see answers that are so wondrous, so far beyond anything we have ever imagined, that our faith is strengthened and stretched to incomparable heights. Our hearts fill with praises and thanksgiving to our wonderful and glorious Lord. He has allowed us to be participants in, or spectators of, these magnificent demonstrations of His omnipotence. We have experienced such encounters on several recent occasions.

There is one in particular that I hope I will never forget.

At a women's retreat, I was approached by Cindy* who had been in one of the sessions I taught. Some of the things I talked about, she said, had stirred her spirit, and she wondered if I had any time at all to meet with her for prayer. I told her the only possible time would be later that Saturday afternoon when the retreat was over, after we had packed all the leftover books from the book table. It would be fairly late. From experience I knew that for the kind of prayer session I anticipated, we needed to have at least an hour available. It was not something that could be rushed or dealt with in a three-minute prayer standing in the corner, especially not with all the other women milling around.

Cindy indicated that her sister would be coming at about four o'clock to pick her up and take her home. I asked, "Cindy, do you think she would mind meeting with us?" I was already thinking about where we might meet. Florence and I were staying over one more night in the hotel, and the most logical place to meet would be in our room, where fortunately we had an adjoining sitting area. Cindy would need to have someone else there with her. Cindy called her sister and returned ten minutes later with a smile on her face. She had agreed to come at four and was willing to be with us for as long as it took.

When four o'clock came Cindy arrived at the book table and

* Not her real name

introduced her sister to me. When my work at the book table was finished the three of us went up in the elevator to our sitting room. Without wasting time, Cindy began to describe some of the struggles she had been going through. Despite several years of recovery and therapy, she felt that she was still subject to considerable anger. She was an avid Bible student, had taken many courses and was even working toward an advanced degree. But Cindy felt certain she had not experienced the best God had for her, though she was active and effective in several areas of women's ministry in her church. Despite her sincere commitment and earnest efforts to be a good wife, mother and Christian, all was not at rest in her soul. Cindy said she had been raised in a dysfunctional home and was sure there must still be some unresolved scars.

"Is it possible," she wanted to know, "to be completely free of this anger once and for all?"

"Cindy," I answered, "when God heals, He heals the whole person. If He could take away all *my* struggles and my anger, I know He can cleanse and heal yours as well. It is possible, however, that there are some weeds growing in the garden of your life that God intends for you to find and dig up. However," I added, "even though God does miracles, not all healing takes place at one time. Healing is a journey, and He is the Travel Master."

After gaining an understanding of Cindy's needs and desires, I suggested it was time to pray. We could talk all day about the issues, but changes would only take place when we came to the Master. Following our usual practice, I asked Cindy to pray first, telling God exactly what her desires were. I said I would then follow her in prayer, and I advised her in advance that I would take authority over satan and order him out. I was careful to give Cindy no idea of what we might expect or what the Lord might do for her; I simply said we would expect Jesus to do some great work for her. I asked her sister, who was sitting in the chair next to Cindy, to be her silent prayer supporter.

As part of my prayer I said, "Lord Jesus, I ask You to fulfill

Your promise of John 14:21." At the conclusion of it I asked, "Cindy, do you see anything? Is the Lord showing you anything?"

It was only a few seconds before Cindy replied that she saw a meadow...then she was there...then she saw someone sitting on a rock. It was Jesus. He had on a white robe, and His arms were outstretched to her. Cindy was reluctant to go to Him. She didn't think she was worthy.

"Cindy, what does Jesus want you to do?"

"He wants me to come to Him, but I can't do that!"

"Cindy, if Jesus is reaching out to you, He wants you to come to Him." It took some amount of encouragement to get her to move toward Him.

Cindy kept asking "Is this real? Am I making this up or imagining this? I do recognize this meadow, though."

It was a long and laborious process to get Cindy to the point of trusting that what she was experiencing was not fabricated. I suspected that her years of therapy might be leading her mind to interfere in this work of faith and trust. I reassured her, "Cindy, I never told you to go to that meadow or to look for Jesus, did I? I never even knew there was a meadow in your life."

Cindy agreed. At last she was standing in front of Jesus but was still reluctant for Him to touch her. Jesus understood, and He was very patient and gentle, as He always is. He had far more patience than I! The clock was ticking. It was getting later and later, and we had made only a little progress. Nevertheless, He granted me a measure of His patience, and we continued.

"Cindy, is there anything you would like to ask Jesus?"

"I can talk to Him? I can ask Him for something?" Cindy was still in a state of uncertainty.

"Cindy, didn't you want to ask Jesus to take away your anger?" I looked over at Cindy's sister. Her eyes were closed, but I could see that she was alert and praying. Occasionally she would look over at Cindy. I repeated, "Cindy, why don't you ask Jesus now if He will take away your anger?"

"Jesus, will You please take away my anger?"

As I described in an earlier chapter, what most frequently happens is that when asked, Jesus will reach His hand into a man's, woman's or child's chest and remove the ugly black stuff and then throw it away. This time, however, Jesus reached His arm around behind Cindy on her left side. Cindy said she could feel something leaving from her lower back.

Jesus showed to me both His incredible sensitivity and His omniscience by not reaching into Cindy's chest. I realized later that Jesus surely had known that Cindy had suffered some early trauma. With her questioning and suspicious mind-set, removing the anger from her chest might very well have created a feeling of revictimization. Jesus is so gentle and caring. He had other ways to perform His spiritual surgery.

Cindy finally felt secure and allowed herself to be held in His loving arms. After a few more moments Jesus took His leave of Cindy but not before affirming to her, "I will never leave you. I will always be here when you need Me."

When Cindy opened her eyes, amazed, relieved and released, well over an hour had slipped by. "Cindy," I asked, "when Jesus removed the anger from your back, did you see what He did with it?" Since I see nothing during these periods, I rely only on the information that is reported to me. A few of our prayer ministers, however, are actually able to see in the spirit what is taking place! On them lies an especially heavy responsibility to say nothing that might be suggestive.

"No," Cindy replied, "I guess He just dropped it on the ground. I did see the black stuff, but I didn't see what He did with it."

Then came the second miracle. Cindy's sister spoke up for the first time. I was not prepared for what she said.

"I saw what He did with it because I was there watching. I saw everything that happened. Cindy couldn't see because she wasn't facing in that direction. But I was standing there off to the side and behind her. I saw Jesus throw it into the clump of trees on the other side that she couldn't see. But that's not all. While Cindy was standing there, Jesus walked over to me. I wasn't afraid. He looked so kind and gentle. Without saying a word, He reached into my chest too and took out a big glob of the same kind of ugly black stuff and threw it into the woods. I just can't believe what I have just experienced. I feel so much lighter and freer. I can't believe it! This is amazing!"

Cindy's sister went on to reassure Cindy that everything she had experienced was real and had actually happened. She too had seen it with her own eyes. I didn't have to do the reassuring. Cindy's sister did it for me. She had been there in that meadow, too!

After a few more minutes of confirmation and encouragement, I warned Cindy that within twenty-four hours satan might try to steal away her healing by telling her she had only imagined it, that it had never really happened. I was so glad Cindy's sister had been there. As uncertain as Cindy might have been, Cindy's sister was equally certain.

Florence heard all the exclamations of enthusiasm from the bedroom and came in to share in the joy. Cindy was thankful, and her sister was exuberant! Before they left, they gave both of us a big emotional hug.

Two sisters transformed by the healing power of the Lord Jesus walked out of our hotel room that afternoon. He had brought healing and joy not to one, but to two at one time!

20

The Proof of
the Resurrection

A SURVEY CONDUCTED by the Barna Research Group, a conservative Christian organization in Glendale, California, finds that 30 percent of "born-again" Christians do not believe that Jesus "came back to physical life after He was crucified."[1] Is it any wonder that if believing Christians have not settled the truth of Jesus' resurrection in their own hearts, liberal theologians and biblical scholars would be working diligently to try to disprove the reality of the Christ of the Bible?

Over the past five years, scholars have published more than two dozen books and scores of footnoted articles, initiating a fierce debate over the risen Jesus. In their relentless search for the historical Jesus, various biblical scholars argue that the gospel stories of the empty tomb and Jesus' post-resurrection appearances are fictions devised long after His death to justify claims of His divinity. In reviewing the claims of these so-called biblical scholars, *Newsweek* magazine states:

> As the apostle Paul insisted, the risen Christ is the cen-
> ter of the Christian faith, the mystery without which
> there would be no church, no hope of eternal life, no
> living Christ to encounter...of no other historical figure
> has the claim been made persistently that God has
> raised him from the dead.
>
> And yet, if the New Testament is to be believed, it
> was the appearance of the resurrected Christ that lit
> the flame of the Christian faith, and the power of the
> Holy Spirit that fired a motley band of fearful disci-
> ples to proclaim the risen Jesus throughout the
> Greco-Roman world.[2]

Is there one of us who at some time in his or her Christian
experience has not questioned the reality of the resurrection as
well as some of the other foundations of our faith? It is that very
word *faith* upon which so much of what we know to be Christian
or biblical truth must rest. There are certain things we can test
logically, scientifically and experientially. But there remain certain mysteries that we simply must accept by faith.

Everything in the Scriptures that I have been able to test (and
I was for many years, to varying degrees, a skeptic) has proven
to be trustworthy. Therefore I have no trouble now accepting
those things that I must accept by faith. The Scriptures themselves tell us that "faith is the substance of things hoped for, the
evidence of things not seen"[3] and "Through faith we understand...without faith it is impossible to please him: for he that
cometh to God must believe."[4]

The more time I spend with Him, the more wondrous demonstrations of His incomprehensible power and ability He shows to
me. What then must be the result for my faith? It grows and
grows until I reach the point where no man could ever convince
me logically or otherwise that the Lord Jesus is not everything
He says He is in the Scriptures.

> A natural man does not accept the things of the Spirit
> of God; for they are foolishness to him, and he cannot
> understand them (1 Cor. 2:14).

> God is spirit; and those who worship Him must wor-
> ship in Spirit and truth (John 4:24).

In the last chapter I mentioned Fran and the wonderful healing Jesus gave her from the years of grief and guilt caused by
her ill-advised abortion. A few months ago during my own personal prayer time, I asked the Lord a question about Fran. Here
is the exact question from my written prayers of that day and the
specific word-for-word answer He gave to me.

"Is it time to ask You to bring together the parts that are willing?...Dear Lord, I pray for answers, for wisdom and insight."

(In addition to her abortion trauma, Fran had suffered years of
horrific victimization that had resulted in the emergence of
numerous multiple personalities. She had asked me when reuni-
fication would begin. I said I didn't know, but the Lord knew.
Hence my question to Him.) The answer came that day:

> Yes, My son, you have heard rightly. It is time. The
> next time you have a meeting with [Fran], I would
> have you to pray [Fran] into My presence. I will meet
> her there on the side of a hill. We will call all the parts
> to Me. Some will be reluctant and hesitate, some will
> refuse, and I will not force them, but many will come
> to Me, and I will direct them to be one. You bring
> [Fran] to Me, and I will send the parts to her that they
> may be one, even as you and I are one. Thus saith the
> Lord thy God...

This answer from the Lord to my prayer request was on
Saturday, December 2, 1995, at about 2:30 P.M. Note where the
Lord said He would meet Fran: on the side of a hill. Two days
later on Monday, December 4, I had my next phone appointment
with Fran at 7:30 P.M.

After we visited for a while and discussed the questions on Fran's mind, I suggested that we pray. I said not a word to Fran about my conversation with the Lord, His answer, or what our requests or focus in prayer would be on this evening. The phone dialogue we had after we prayed follows in part.

"Fran, what do you see? Do you see anything?"

"I see an ocean. Oh! I love oceans!"

"What else do you see?"

"There's a hill there, also; it runs down to the ocean."

Silently in my heart I shouted, *Yes! Thank You, Lord Jesus!* Have you ever shouted silently in your heart? Can you imagine the excitement I was feeling? Jesus had told me two days before He would meet Fran on the side of a hill. Fran knew nothing about His words to me. I was eager to ask the next question. "Do you see anything on the hill?"

"Yes, I do. There's a group of people over there. It looks like a group of children, and there's a central figure in the center of them."

"Do you recognize that central figure at all?"

"Well, yes, it has to be Jesus!"

Yes, it *was* Jesus Fran was seeing once again in the spirit, and it was not long before approximately thirty little girls were reunited into Fran. There were others who were unsure and hesitant, just as Jesus had said. But a major work took place that evening — just as Jesus had said.

Is this story awesome to you? It is true, exactly as I have repeated it to you. What did the Lord Jesus do for my faith that evening? He cemented it even more securely on a solid rock from which no force on earth can dislodge it! My faith was strong already. I believe in prayer. I believe in the power of the risen Lord Jesus Christ. But to have Him tell me two days earlier what He was going to do and then to see Him carry out His proclamation was like nothing I had ever experienced before!

I have compassion for the seventy-five so-called scholars who formed the provocative Jesus Seminar and who argue that little of the New Testament can be trusted. They set themselves up as experts, and they vote upon which parts of the Scriptures can be trusted and which parts must be discounted. Imagine voting on God, as if that would make any difference or determine His efficacy!

Do they not understand that "God is a Spirit: and those who worship Him must worship in spirit and truth"?[5] Do they not understand that "a natural man does not accept the things of the Spirit of God; for they are foolishness to him and he cannot understand them, because they are spiritually appraised"?[6] Have they not read that "he that believeth not the Son shall not see life; but the wrath of God abideth on him"?[7] Do they not understand that the entire Christian faith is based on just that: faith? "Without faith it is impossible to please Him."[8]

The resurrection of the Lord Jesus Christ is not an issue for debate. First, it is an historical fact. Second, it is proven by the transformation in the lives of those who believe. What other force or power could have worked the wondrous changes in your own life?

The prince of darkness strives to infiltrate the minds of lethargic or even careless Christians to cause them to listen to the naysayers and to doubt the truth. Stand against him! Exercise the authority the Lord Jesus has given you,[9] bind and banish him, and in the name of the Lord Jesus Christ cast him out from your presence. To see satan flee, as the Bible says he will,[10] is enough to further establish your faith that Jesus lives. Reminder: Do it aloud (but not loudly) with authority. Do it daily, even when you are not sensing his attack or infiltration. "Now you know this truth; how happy you will be if you put it into practice!"[11]

Third, the resurrection of the Lord Jesus Christ is proven by the clear and valid evidence that He did appear, does appear, and as a living Lord, will appear to you today as He has to countless hundreds that we know and thousands of others as well. I have seen the Lord Jesus. You can, too. You can be touched by the Master and experience the miracle healing power of seeing Jesus!

Notes

Chapter 1
The Encounter in Nashville

1. The story of Willa is totally true. Only the names and places have been changed to protect family members who still have no knowledge of her experience.
2. Dyslexia is an inability to read and to assimilate or organize facts.
3. Both books are published by Thomas Nelson Publishers, Nashville, Tennessee.

Chapter 2
"That Was Jesus, All Right!"

1. "No temptation [trial or testing] has overtaken you but such as is common to man [woman or child]; and God is faithful, who will not allow you to be [tested] beyond what you are able, but with the [testing] will provide the way of escape also, that you may be able to endure it" (1 Cor. 10:13).
2. Arlys Norcross McDonald, *Repressed Memories* (Grand Rapids, Mich.: Revell, 1995).
3. 1 Thess. 5:18.
4. Since her dramatic and perhaps miraculous healing, the Lord has given Willa her own ministry of praying with others for healing. He has also given her the unique gift of being able to see in the spirit what others are seeing in the spirit. She is aware of what they are going to see before they see it. She is extremely cautious, however, never to suggest to them or tell them what she sees. This is of the greatest importance.
5. John 14:21, KJV.

Chapter 3
"I Have Seen the Lord"

1. See Mark 16:1.
2. See John 19:30.
3. See Matt. 27:45,51 and Mark 15:33,38.
4. See John 19:38-42.
5. See Mark 16:3.
6. See Matt. 28:1-4 and Mark 16:6.
7. Matt. 28:5-6.
8. See Matt. 28:7.
9. See John 20:2.
10. John 2:19.
11. See John 20:1-13.
12. See John 20:15-16.
13. See John 20:16. In Hebrew *rabboni* is the highest title of honor. It may be translated "my great master."
14. See John 20:17 and Matthew 28:10.
15. See John 20:18.
16. See Luke 24:18-21.
17. See Luke 24:22-35.
18. See John 20:19 and Luke 24:38-39.
19. See Luke 24:40-48, 50-51.
20. 1 Cor. 15:1,3-5, emphasis added.
21. See John 20:24-25,27-29.
22. See John 21:1-11.

Chapter 4
How Can This Be?

1. Spiros Zodhiates, *The Complete Word Study Dictionary* (Chattanooga, Tenn.: AMG Publishers, 1992).
2. This term, seeing Jesus in the spirit, has been created from John's words in Revelation 4:2: "Immediately I was *in the Spirit*; and behold, a throne was standing in heaven, and One sitting on the throne" (emphasis added).
3. For the story of my discovery and recovery of repressed memories, please see chapters 2 and 3 in my book *Wake Up, Men!* (Dallas, Tex.: Word, 1994).
4. One of the many rewarding facts of praying someone into His presence is the consistency of the things that are said and seen. Once a

person has seen His outstretched arms, as frequently happens, he or she invariably says, "He wants me to come to Him!"

5. John 20:28-29.

Chapter 5
Divine Timing

1. No, the small *s* on satan is not a typographical mistake. Although a capital letter is proper English form, it is also a sign of honor and respect, and he doesn't deserve any!

2. Michael's story and letter as well as his wife, Donna's, story and letter (shared in chapter 6) are used with their permission. Names and details have been changed to protect identities.

Chapter 6
No Longer the Least, the Worst and the Last

1. Michael and Donna's story is used with permission. Names and details have been changed to protect identities.

Chapter 7
Jesus Is Alive, and He Really Loves Me

1. Sarah's letter and journal entries are reprinted with permission. Names and details have been changed to protect identities.

Chapter 8
Substantiating Similarities

1. Oswald Chambers, *My Utmost for His Highest* (various publishers), s.v. "June 11."

2. These seven exceptions, when Jesus went to the people who needed Him rather than the other way around, are Jesus' unsolicited healings. They were to demonstrate a point for a particular purpose. For further detail and scriptural citations, see our book *The Promise of Healing* (Nashville, Tenn.: Thomas Nelson, 1994), 193-194.

3. The word *communicant* is often defined as "a church member who is eligible to take communion," particularly in traditional churches. However, I use the word to refer to those whom we are leading to the Lord in prayer so that they can *commune* with Him.

4. John 8:12, KJV.

Chapter 9
Ruth Came to the Garden Alone

1. Ruth's story is included here with her permission; however, names and details have been changed to protect identities.

Chapter 10
Now Her Husband Has a Healthy and Happy Wife

1. Ps. 139:1, TLB.
2. Carol Miller's story about the prayer experience she shared with Monica is told here with Monica's permission. Names and details have been changed to protect identities.

Chapter 12
Guidelines for Praying Someone Into His Presence

1. See John 14:21.
2. See Ps. 139:1-3 and Matt. 6:8.
3. Matt. 23:14.
4. Luke 10:19.

Chapter 13
Blockages to Seeing Jesus in the Spirit

1. Oswald Chambers, *My Utmost for His Highest* (various publishers).
2. James 1:6-7.
3. The questionnaires in chapters 11 and 13 in our book *Get a Life Without the Strife* (Nashville, Tenn.: Thomas Nelson, 1993) will enable you to determine if you are ministering to someone who has been sexually abused as a child (even though there may be no conscious or even fragmented memory of the abuse) or if the person has been used in satanic worship rituals.

Chapter 14
Words of Caution and Answers
to Some of Your Questions

1. The terms *parts* and *alters* refer to the inner personalities of some-

one with MPD, or multiple personality disorder. A coven (group of witches) may create parts or alters within a person for control and obedience purposes. Over the years some of these parts may confess Jesus as their Lord, but many will be adamantly loyal to the coven. Dealing with such coven-loyal parts should not be attempted by a novice but only by one who has vast experience and wisdom regarding the implications in the spiritual realm.

Chapter 15
Other Wondrous Works of the Lord

1. Names and details in Debbie's story have been changed to protect identities. Her letters and poem and her remarkable story are used with her permission.
2. See chapter 18 for suggestions on dealing with attacks of the enemy.
3. See Matt. 6:12-15.

Chapter 16
Jesus Heals a Mother and Then Her Son

1. Names and details in Gwen and Daryl's stories have been changed to protect identities. Their stories are used with permission.

Chapter 17
"There's Nothing More We Can Do for You"

1. Names and details in Kathy's story have been changed to protect identities. Her story is used with permission.

Chapter 18
Be Watchful, Be Vigilant

1. James 4:7, emphasis added.
2. 2 Cor. 11:3, KJV.
3. 2 Cor. 11:14-15.
4. Luke 9:1, KJV.
5. Note that some early writings and today's translations refer to the sending out of "seventy others." There is valid mathematical reason to conclude that the correct figure is actually seventy-two. Luke 9:1 says twelve were sent out; Luke 10:1 says the Lord "appointed seventy-two

others." The two groups total eighty-four sent out altogether with the same empowerment and instructions. The lowest common denominators of eighty-four are seven and twelve, significant numbers in Scripture, representing perfection and administration or completion.

6. Luke 10:1,17, TEV.
7. Luke 10:19-20, KJV.
8. Eph. 6:16.
9. See John 14:27.
10. I clearly differentiate here between the spiritual head and the domestic authority in the home. I strongly believe that only the Lord Jesus can be the authority in the home, and therefore the husband cannot be. Nor can the wife. We are to be one, just as we are one in Christ. For further understanding and scriptural perspectives, see chapter 13, "How Can the Husband Be the Head of the Wife?" in my book *Wake Up, Men!* (Dallas, Tex.: Word, 1994). I hope you will find it interesting and challenging — but I warn you: it *is* different!
11. John 13:17, TEV.

Chapter 19
More Wondrous Works

1. Fran's story is used with permission. Names and details have been changed to protect identities.
2. See 1 Cor. 15:42,44.

Chapter 20
The Proof of the Resurrection

1. Newsweek, 8 April 1996, "Rethinking the Resurrection," 62.
2. Ibid., 61.
3. Heb. 11:1, KJV.
4. Heb. 11:3,6, KJV.
5. John 4:24.
6. 1 Cor. 2:14.
7. John 3:36, KJV.
8. Hebrews 11:6.
9 See Luke 10:19.
10. See James 4:7.
11. John 13:17, TEV.

A Prayer of Authority

In the name of the Lord Jesus Christ,
I rebuke you, satan.
I take authority over you!
I rebuke you; I bind you; I banish you!
I command you to leave this place.
I command you to leave me.
You are not permitted to interfere in my life.
In the name of the Lord Jesus Christ, satan,
I tell you and all your evil spirits to be gone!
Be gone from here!

Make photocopies of this commandment prayer and place them in strategic places in your home and workplace. Use the prayer to rebuke satan daily or whenever you suspect or feel that you are under attack by the enemy.